Classical Five Element
Chinese Astrology
Made Easy

David Twicken, Ph.D., L.Ac.

Writers Club Press
San Jose New York Lincoln Shanghai

Classical Five Element Chinese Astrology Made Easy

Published by Writers Club Press
an imprint of iUniverse.com, Inc.

For information address:
iUniverse.com, Inc.
620 North 48th Street
Suite 201
Lincoln, NE 68504-3467
www.iuniverse.com

Author Contact: WWW.ChineseAstrologyNow.Com

ISBN: 0-595-09408-2

Printed in the United States of America

Table of Contents

Acknowledgments

It is with my deepest gratitude I thank Mr. Gary Lam for sharing his knowledge and experience as a "Tzu Ping" Chinese Astrologer. Thanks to Susan Morse, Dena Saxer and Tim O'Connor, for editing, discussion, inspiration and friendship.

Introduction

What is my destiny? Will marriage, wealth and happiness be abundant? When will romance and prosperity come into my life? These deeply important aspects of life have led people to seek professional fortune-tellers for thousands of years. In Asia, a system of divination evolved which reveals one's destiny, luck and fate. From emperor to common person, it was common practice to consult oracles for guidance; I Ching, Tung Shu-Chinese Almanac, Feng Shui, Palm Readers and Astrologers were consulted for guidance about every aspect of life.

During the ninth century A.D., an extraordinary man, "Tzu Ping Hsu", revolutionized existing systems of Chinese astrology by introducing new and revolutionary applications. His methods were so influential, the astrology community named his enhanced system in his honor, "Tzu Ping Astrology". Tzu Ping astrology is the most common form of astrology practiced throughout Asia. It is a highly accurate divination system for predicting fortune, luck, personality, health, romance, marriage, wealth, family relations and karmic conditions.

The common usage of *Chinese* Astrology in the western community has been evaluating attributes of the Chinese Zodiac animals. This analysis captures the *birth year* aspect of a person's life. It does not include the Hour, Day, Month or future cycles of time. In Tzu Ping astrology, all cycles of time are evaluated to obtain a complete picture of a person and his or her life path.

Calculating a birth chart or "Four Pillars" is the initial step in performing a Tzu Ping Astrological analysis. This information is obtained from the ancient 10,000 Year Chinese Calendar. This calendar includes the influence of each Hour, Day, Month and Year. Because the complete Chinese calendar has been largely inaccessible in the West, the deepest aspects of Chinese Astrology have not been revealed. A *Chinese Astrology Calendar* consists of three major parts: Stems, Branches and Solar months. Because this information can be difficult to obtain, I have developed an English translation of the Chinese Calendar, "Chinese Astrology Calendar Made Easy ©". This calendar is user-friendly, allowing easy access to the deepest levels of Tzu Ping Astrology. In a short period of time you will be able to construct a Four Pillars birth chart in less than 60 seconds.

This book was written with user friendliness as a primary feature. It includes many examples to reinforce every concept and technique. Located at the end of each chapter is an example summarizing and applying the chapter's topic. Following each example carefully is the key to understanding this material. The key to learning this ancient system is the chapter on Five Elements. The Five Elements are the foundation to this system. With a strong understanding of the Five Elements, you are prepared to deeply understand this powerful system of divination. Welcome to the fascinating world of Tzu Ping, Chinese Astrology!

Chapter 1

Life Force

Chinese Astrologers view the universe as filled with energy; an energy which moves through endless flows of transformation. This energy comprises all of life; including Stars, Planets, Trees, Mountains, Water, Animals and Human Life. The ancient Chinese called this energy Qi. Qi is both matter and energy. It is also the force which allows a transformation from energy to matter and matter to energy. For example, Water is a type of Qi; and is a perfect example of how Qi transforms. Water can be in the form of ice, ice can transform into Water, and Water into steam. Qi is ice, Qi is Water, Qi is steam and Qi is the heat which allows the transformation to occur. Qi is all of life. It takes form to become the densest substances and is also contained in the subtlest of substances. Every part of the universe is a blend of different types of Qi. To understand this blending of Qi is to understand Chinese Astrology. To understand Qi is to understand life. Knowing the rhythms and expressions of Qi, is to be able to predict and change life.

All tools used in Tzu Ping astrology are variations of Qi. This book will introduce you to Yin-Yang, Five Elements, Stems, Branches and cycles of time, they are different aspects or transformations of Qi. These tools help calculate the effects of Qi on a given person throughout a lifetime. Chinese Astrology is the study of Qi!

Chapter 2

Yin-Yang

From the beginning of time, mankind has searched to understand the Heavens, Earth and Human life, whether it be Hindus in India, Aztecs in Mexico, Jews of Israel or the ancient Egyptians. In China, a model of understanding nature evolved which would become the roots of Chinese philosophy, Medicine, Nutrition, Martial Arts, Feng Shui and Astrology. This system is Yin-Yang. Yin-Yang theory includes viewing the Universe as one integrated whole, as well as two opposing, but interdependent elements. All aspects of life can be categorized into Yin-Yang. For example, Heaven-Earth, Man-Woman, Hot-Cold, Left-Right, Light-Dark, Front-Back, Hard-Soft, North-South, East-West, Root-Branch, Top-Bottom and Fast-Quick are two sides of one phenomenon. Yin-Yang theory categories any situation into two parts. This is the key to Yin-Yang theory, each part gives life to its opposite. There must be a Left to have Right, a Strong to have Weak, a Front to have Back. They are not two separate entities, but two sides of the same coin. They give life to each other, never being separate.

Yin-Yang is a predominant component in Chinese Astrology. One major application of Yin-Yang theory is Yang represents a growing or expanding phase, and Yin, a declining phase. All of life flows through this basic model of rising and declining. Each expansion leads to a decline, which leads to another expansion and another decline, in an endless cycle. In Tzu Ping astrology, the first step is determining the strength of the Birth Chart or Self. The "Self", which represents a person, will be categorized as one of the Five Elements and named either Yang Wood, Yin Wood, Yang Water, Yin Water, Yang Fire, Yin Fire, Yang Earth, Yin Earth, Yang Metal or Yin Metal. This will be explained in the next two chapters. Yin-Yang will permeate every aspect of Tzu Ping Astrology.

Chapter 3

Five Elements

Five Elements are the basis or foundation of Tzu Ping Astrology. They are the ABC's of calculating, evaluating and applying the knowledge of Four Pillars astrology. They are the key to comprehending Tzu Ping Astrology!

A circle can be viewed as one integrated whole.

This circle represent the oneness of life.

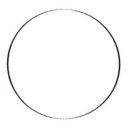

A circle can also be viewed as two parts, left and right. These are Yin-Yang.

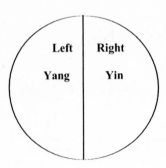

This same circle can be viewed with five segments. These are the Five Elements.

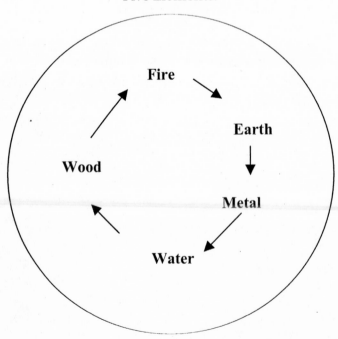

This circle is segmented into five parts, with each segment assigned an element: Water, Wood, Fire, Earth and Metal. Each element holds a position within the circle. For example, Wood is positioned where the circle begins to move upward and represents growth or spring time. Fire is located where the portion of the circle reaches its peak, symbolizing summer; Earth is positioned where harvesting takes place, and represents indian summer; Metal represents turning inward or contraction, and represents autumn, and Water is where the circle turns completely inward to regenerate, representing winter. Water also portrays preparation for a new spring, wood or growth cycle. This cycle continues infinitely and reflects self-generation and the eternal nature of life.

The relative position of each of Five Elements or Five Phases in the circle determines its specific relationship with each of the other elements. For example, Water is the mother to Wood, grandparent to Fire, grandchild of Earth and child of Metal. Each element has those distinct relationships with the four remaining elements. The ability to apply those relationships is crucial to Chinese Astrology. Table 1 summarizes these relationships.

Table 1

Element ➡	Water	Wood	Fire	Earth	Metal
Parent	Metal	Water	Wood	Fire	Earth
Sibling—Same	Water	Wood	Fire	Earth	Metal
Child—Offspring	Wood	Fire	Earth	Metal	Water
Grandchild	Fire	Earth	Metal	Water	Wood
Grandparent Controller	Earth	Metal	Water	Wood	Fire

How to interpret this chart.

Water's parent is Metal.
Water's sibling is Water.
Water's child is Wood.
Water's grandchild is Fire.
Water's Controller is Earth.

From these four relationships we see four key interactions.

1. Each element gives to another element. The parent.
2. Each element controls another element. The grandparent or controller.
3. Each element is controlled by another element. The grandchild.
4. Each element receives from another element. The child.
5. Each element is supported by another element. The same or sibling.

These relationships are expressed in the actions of giving, receiving, controlling and being controlled. The key to a natural healthy life is to find the proper balance of these actions.

One action is not better than another, there is meaning only when a situation is compared to a particular birth chart. Some people need to be nourished, other's need control, and still other's need to give. What is beneficial is relative to the condition of the Day Stem.

Each of the relationships can be balanced, excessive or deficient. Four Pillar Astrology is a tool which analyzes how the universe created the Five Elements at birth. Upon evaluating the strengths and weaknesses of a birth chart, one can calculate how Five Element cycles of time affect a person. It is future cycles; Hours, Days, Months, Years and 10 Year cycles which are used for predictions. It is the future cycles which will provide the Five Element energies necessary to provide balance, opportunities or challenges.

Table 2 has the major actions used in Five Element Astrology. They create the foundation for all remedies.

Table 2

Situation	First Action	Second Action
Weakness	Nourish. Add the Parent Element. Add same or Sibling element.	Add a small amount of the Grandparent element to make the Mother stronger when appropriate.
Too Strong or Excessive	Control. Add the Grandparent.	Reduce. Add the Child element to take from the overly strong parent. It will drain it.

The following diagrams illustrate how each element is affected by the four other elements in the five element system and which elements are necessary to balance a situation. Determine which elements are needed when an excess or weakness exists. Confirm your choices with Table 3 below.

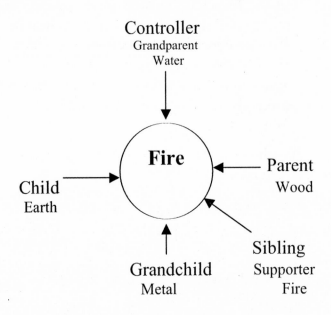

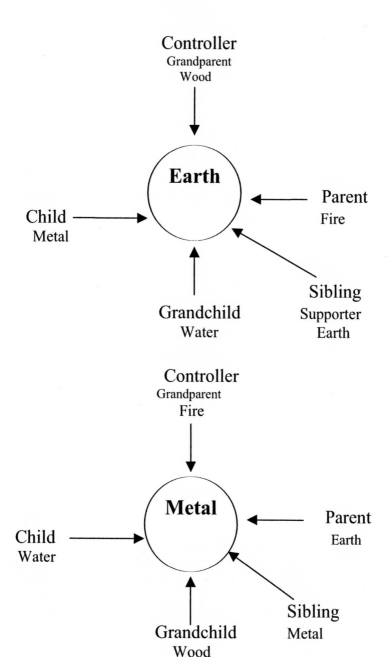

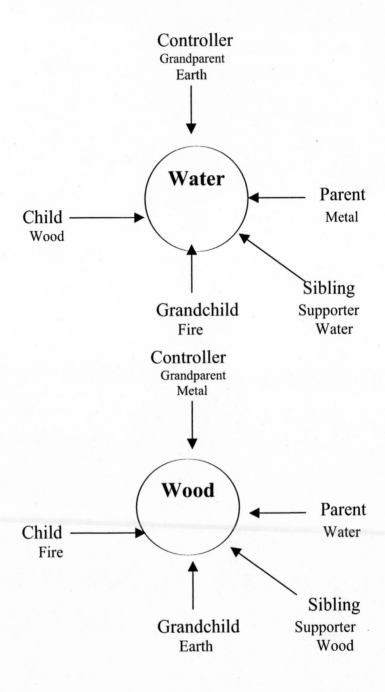

Table 3

Element	Corrections for Excess	Corrections for Weakness
Water	Earth, Wood	Metal, Water
Wood	Metal, Fire	Water, Wood
Fire	Water, Earth	Wood, Fire
Earth	Wood, Metal	Fire, Earth
Metal	Fire, Water	Earth, Metal

The actual determination of the condition of a birth chart is explained in Chapter 11. For now it is important to know which elements are needed during excess and deficient conditions.

The Five Elements interact in a variety of ways. Two major cycles are the promotion and controlling cycles. These two cycles provide the basis for most applications of "Tzu Ping" Astrology. The following explains these two cycles.

The Promotion cycle is the Parent to Child relationship within the Five Elements. The following illustrates the Promotion cycle.

Promotion Cycle

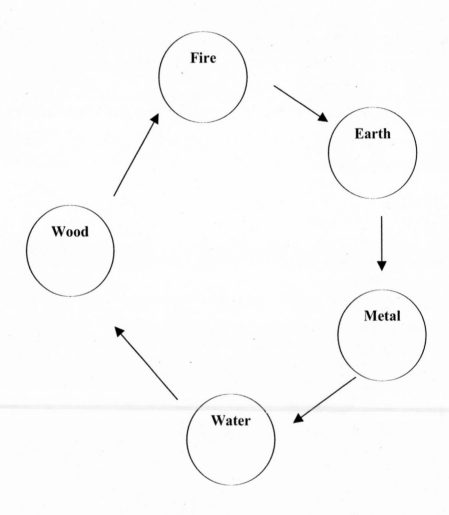

Promotion Cycle

1. If Water is placed on Wood, it will grow. Water is the mother of Wood.
2. If Wood is placed in a Fire, Fire will grow. Wood is the mother of Fire.
3. Fire will turn substances into Ashes or Earth. Fire is the Mother of Earth.
4. Metal is found from Earth. Earth is the Mother of Metal.
5. Metal can be liquefied into Water. Metal is the Mother of Water.

The controlling cycle is the grandparent to child relationship. The following illustrates the controlling cycle.

Controlling Cycle

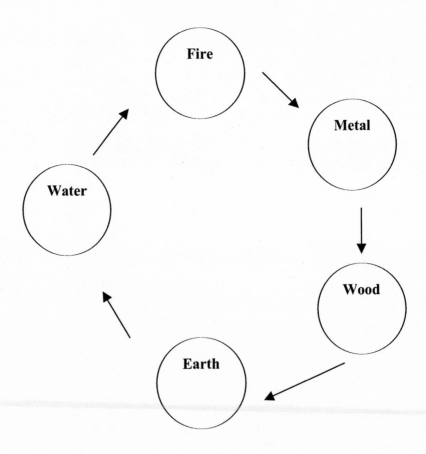

Controlling Cycle

1. Fire burns Metal or controls Metal. Grandparent relationship.
2. Metal cuts Wood or controls Wood. Grandparent relationship.
3. Wood absorbs nutrients from the Earth and controls Earth. Grandparent relationship.
4. Earth absorbs Water or controls Water. Grandparent relationship.
5. Water puts out the Fire and controls Fire. Grandparent relationship.

Use the Promotion and Controlling cycle diagrams to determine the relationship between any Five Elements. After a short period of time you will memorize these relationships.

Chapter 4

Energy Cycles

Chinese astrology is a marvelous illustration of our relationship to nature. Tzu Ping astrology is a systematic method of calculating nature's influences on woman and man. The Application of Yin-Yang, Five Elements and cycles of time provides the vehicle for calculating a birth chart, which reflects the natal or constitutional condition. This birth chart is called "Four Pillars".

Classical Tzu Ping astrology is based on the influences of time. Time includes Hours, Days, Months, Years and 10 Year cycles. As with all of life, time can be categorized into Yin-Yang; Yang is a Heavenly Stem and Yin, an Earthly Branch. Heavenly Stems reflect Yang or Heaven's influence, Earthly Branches represent Yin or Earth's influences.

Cycles of time are also categorized into Five Elements. The Five Elements are Water, Wood, Fire, Earth and Metal. Each element contains a Yin and Yang aspect, for example, Yang Wood, Yin Wood, Yang Water and Yin Water. The 10 Heavenly Stems are the Yin-Yang aspect of the Five Elements. They are Yang Wood, Yin Wood, Yang Fire, Yin Fire, Yang Earth, Yin Earth, Yang Metal, Yin Metal, Yang Water, Yin Water.

The 12 Earthly Branches are the Five Elements with their Yin-Yang quality, totaling 10 Branches. They also have an additional

Earth element, making 12 total elements. Earth is a transformer which can transform one element or season into another. That is why there are two extra Earth elements, one Yin and one Yang. (This will be explained throughout the book). The 12 Branches are Yang Wood, Yin Wood, Yang Earth, Yang Fire, Yin Fire, Yin Earth, Yang Metal, Yin Metal, Yang Earth, Yin Water Yang Water, Yin Earth. Notice the Earth Branches are between changes from one element to another. Branches can also be referred to by their Chinese Zodiac Animal name. (See Table 4).

Stems and Branches represent a flow of energy; each Hour, Day, Month and Year is made up of one combination of a Stem and Branch. Each specific Stem and Branch combination is called a Binomial. Binomials are organized in a cycle of 60, which includes every combination of Stems and Branches. Six cycles of 10 Stems and five cycles of 12 Branches equals one cycle of 60. Hours, Days, Months and Years contain those Stem and Branch energy combinations. *Table 4 contains the 60 binomial cycle.* A birth chart has four Binomials, one Binomial for the Hour, Day, Month and Year. Those four units of time create a birth chart, which is called the Four Pillars. The Four Pillars are the foundation for Classical Five Element Chinese Astrology. In Table 4, binomial one includes Yang Wood, number two has Yin Wood and the Five Elements continue until Binomial 10. Yang Wood reappears again at 11, 21, 31, 41 and 51. The 10 Stems continue for six cycles, completing a cycle of 60. The Branch Rat, begins at number 1 and the 12 Animals or Branches continue until they repeat again with the Rat, at 13, 25, 37 and 49.

Table 4

Stem and Branch Cycle of 60
For Hours, Days, Months and Years

Number	1	2	3	4	5	6
Stem	Yang Wood	Yin Wood	Yang Fire	Yin Fire	Yang Earth	Yin Earth
Branch	Rat	Ox	Tiger	Rabbit	Dragon	Snake
Number	7	8	9	10	11	12
Stem	Yang Metal	Yin Metal	Yang Water	Yin Water	Yang Wood	Yin Wood
Branch	Horse	Sheep	Monkey	Cock	Dog	Pig
Number	13	14	15	16	17	18
Stem	Yang Fire	Yin Fire	Yang Earth	Yin Earth	Yang Metal	Yin Metal
Branch	Rat	Ox	Tiger	Rabbit	Dragon	Snake
Number	19	20	21	22	23	24
Stem	Yang Water	Yin Water	Yang Wood	Yin Wood	Yang Fire	Yin Fire
Branch	Horse	Sheep	Monkey	Cock	Dog	Pig
Number	25	26	27	28	29	30
Stem	Yang Earth	Yin Earth	Yang Metal	Yin Metal	Yang Water	Yin Water
Branch	Rat	Ox	Tiger	Rabbit	Dragon	Snake
Number	31	32	33	34	35	36
Stem	Yang Wood	Yin Wood	Yang Fire	Yin Fire	Yang Earth	Yin Earth
Branch	Horse	Sheep	Monkey	Cock	Dog	Pig
Number	37	38	39	40	41	42
Stem	Yang Metal	Yin Metal	Yang Water	Yin Water	Yang Wood	Yin Wood
Branch	Rat	Ox	Tiger	Rabbit	Dragon	Snake
Number	43	44	45	46	47	48
Stem	Yang Fire	Yin Fire	Yang Earth	Yin Earth	Yang Metal	Yin Metal
Branch	Horse	Sheep	Monkey	Cock	Dog	Pig
Number	49	50	51	52	53	54
Stem	Yang Water	Yin Water	Yang Wood	Yin Wood	Yang Fire	Yin Fire
Branch	Rat	Ox	Tiger	Rabbit	Dragon	Snake
Number	55	56	57	58	59	60
Stem	Yang Earth	Yin Earth	Yang Metal	Yin Metal	Yang Water	Yin Water
Branch	Horse	Sheep	Monkey	Cock	Dog	Pig

Branch	Pig	Rat	Ox	Tiger	Rabbit	Dragon	Snake	Horse	Sheep	Monkey	Cock	Dog
Main Element	Yang Water	Yin Water	Yin Earth	Yang Wood	Yin Wood	Yang Earth	Yang Fire	Yin Fire	Yin Earth	Yang Metal	Yin Metal	Yang Earth

The small box above reflects the main element for each of the Branches or animals.

The Heavenly Stems are in the top row and represent heavenly or Yang influence. They are always named as a Five Element: for example, Yang Wood, Yin Wood, Yang Fire or Yin Fire. The lower row contains Earthly Branches or Chinese Zodiac animals. They can be named as a Five Element or as an Animal. I recommend using the Animal name, because it helps differentiate the Branches from the Stems, especially since there are four Earthly Branches. Either system can be utilized. The 60 Binomials include every possible energy combination; each Hour, Day, Month and Year has a Binomial.

The diagram below is the Four Pillars. It is the foundation for a "Tzu Ping" Five Element Astrological analysis. From the Chinese calendar, a Stem and Branch is placed in the Hour, Day, Month and Year Pillars.

Four Pillars

Hour	Day	Month	Year
Stem	Stem	Stem	Stem
Branch Animal	Branch Animal	Branch Animal	Branch Animal

Chapter 5

Branches or Chinese Zodiac Animals

Diagram 1, illustrates the 12 Branches and their corresponding main element, Chinese Zodiac animal, geographical location, and order of Branches. This diagram assists in understanding many of the interactions of two or more animals.

The Branches or animals in the same geographical area have an affinity with each other. They share the same element and therefore like each other. There is also a Trinity or Harmonic relation between each fourth Animal or Branch which creates a positive relationship. For example, Cock, Ox and Snake are four places apart from each other, and therefore are compatible. The cardinal or middle positions also have a special relationship with their opposite cardinal position. The Cock and Rabbit, and Rat and Horse, oppose each other creating a spark, causing excitement and possible romance, as well as friction and difficulties. Combinations between Animals or Branches will be discussed in Chapter 13.

Diagram 1

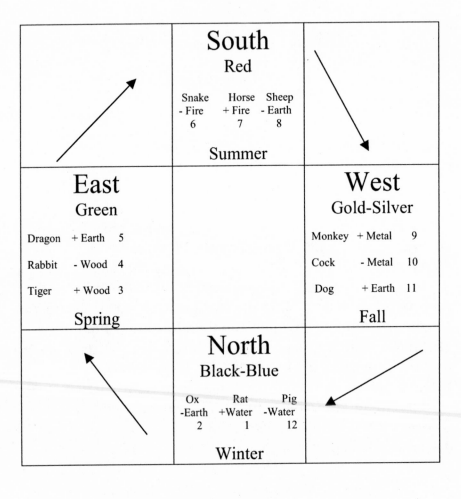

	South Red Snake Horse Sheep - Fire + Fire - Earth 6 7 8 Summer	
East Green Dragon + Earth 5 Rabbit - Wood 4 Tiger + Wood 3 Spring		**West** Gold-Silver Monkey + Metal 9 Cock - Metal 10 Dog + Earth 11 Fall
	North Black-Blue Ox Rat Pig -Earth +Water -Water 2 1 12 Winter	

Branch—Animal Relationships

Table 5 summarizes the major relationships of the Branches or Animals. Each Branch has an Animal name, corresponding main element, season, time of day and direction. This information is used to calculate specific elemental influences affecting a person, these will be discussed throughout the book.

Table 5

Animal	Main Element	Season	Time of Day	Direction
Pig	Yang Water	Winter	9pm-11pm	North
Rat	Yin Water	Winter	11pm-1am	North
Ox	Yin Earth	Winter	1am-3am	North
Tiger	Yang Wood	Spring	3am-5am	East
Rabbit	Yin Wood	Spring	5am-7am	East
Dragon	Yang Earth	Spring	7am-9am	East
Snake	Yang Fire	Summer	9am-11am	South
Horse	Yin Fire	Summer	11am-1pm	South
Sheep	Yin Earth	Summer	1pm-3pm	South
Monkey	Yang Metal	Fall	3pm-5pm	West
Cock	Yin Metal	Fall	5pm-7pm	West
Dog	Yang Earth	Fall	7pm-9pm	West

Finding Branch Gender

Finding Branch gender or polarity, which is determining whether a Branch is Yin or Yang, is an integral aspect in Astrology. There are two major methods of determining the gender of each Animal. The first is the Outer method and the Second is the Inner Method. The Outer method determines the polarity of the Birth Year. This assists in calculating 10 Year Luck Cycles. The gender determines the direction of the Stem and Branch flow, this will be explained in the "10 Year Luck Cycles" chapter. The Inner method also identifies a Yin-Yang nature of each Branch, this method is used for all other applications of Tzu Ping astrology. For example, the Horse and Snake are both Fire, for Inner method calculations, the Horse is Yin Fire and the Snake is Yang fire; for Outer method calculations, Snake is Yin Fire and the Horse is Yang Fire. It is very important to know whether an Animal is Yin or Yang.

Outer Method

In Diagram 1, the main element reflects the Outer method for calculating the Yin-Yang aspect of each Animal or Branch. The concept of numbers and Yin-Yang can explain this method. Each Branch has a number, for example, the Rat is 1, Ox-2, Tiger-3, Rabbit-4, Dragon-5, Snake-6, Horse-7, Sheep-8, Monkey-9, Cock-10, Dog-11 and Pig 12, (Diagram 1). Odd numbers are Yang and even numbers are Yin. When finding the polarity or Yin-Yang nature of the Birth Year, use this Outer or external method. Diagram 1, reflects this outer approach. It also reflects the gender of a person. The+sign means Yang and the—sign means Yin. For example, if a person was born in a Cock year, they are *Yin* Metal (Cock). If the person is a woman, she is a *Yin Female*, if a man, a *Yin male*.

Diagram 1

Outer Method

	South	
↗	**South** Red Snake　Horse　Sheep - Fire　+ Fire　- Earth 6　　7　　8 Summer	↘
East Green Dragon　+ Earth　5 Rabbit　- Wood　4 Tiger　+ Wood　3 Spring		**West** Gold-Silver Monkey　+ Metal　9 Cock　　- Metal　10 Dog　　+ Earth　11 Fall
↖	**North** Black-Blue Ox　　Rat　　Pig - Earth　+ Water　- Water 2　　1　　12 Winter	↙

Internal Method

In most applications of Tzu Ping Astrology, the internal method is used. Each of the "Pure" animals, all animals except the four Earths (Ox, Dragon, Sheep and Dog) are Yin-Yang pairs. The Earths are transformers from one season to another, and are not considered "pure" aspects of their cardinal position. They are mixtures of numerous elements and a unifying force. This will be explained throughout the book. For each geographical location, there is a pair of pure branches, the first animal is Yang and the second is Yin. Odd numbers are Yang and even numbers are Yin. For example, the North contains Pig-Rat, East contains Tiger-Rabbit, South contains Snake-Horse and West contains Monkey-Cock. The Pig, Tiger, Snake and Monkey are all Yang and the Rat, Rabbit, Horse and Cock are Yin. (See Diagram 2). This formula is used in all calculations, *except* the Yin-Yang gender of the Birth Year.

Diagram 2

Internal Method

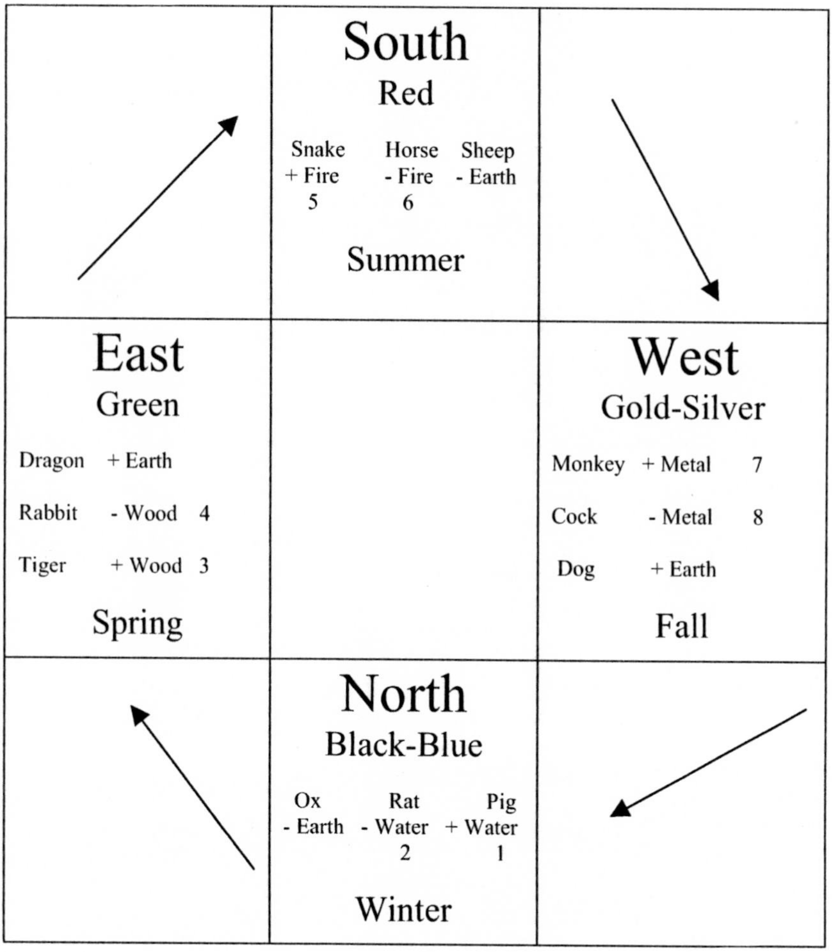

	South	
	Red	
	Snake Horse Sheep + Fire - Fire - Earth 5 6	
	Summer	
East		West
Green		Gold-Silver
Dragon + Earth		Monkey + Metal 7
Rabbit - Wood 4		Cock - Metal 8
Tiger + Wood 3		Dog + Earth
Spring		Fall
	North	
	Black-Blue	
	Ox Rat Pig - Earth - Water + Water 2 1	
	Winter	

Hidden Elements

Nine of the 12 Branches or Animals contain "Hidden Elements". These are minor elements contained inside a Branch. The Hidden Elements influence each person and must be evaluated. The following chart shows the Hidden Elements contained in each Animal or Branch. The bottom of each page in the Chinese Astrology Calendar Made Easy has a box showing the main and Hidden elements for each Animal. These elements represent the Internal Method and are used for all calculations *except* the polarity for the Year of Birth Animal, which is used to calculate 10 Year Luck Cycles.

Hidden Elements

Animal	Main Element	Hidden Element
Pig	Yang Water	Yang Wood
Rat	Yin Water	
Ox	Yin Earth	Yin Water, Yin Metal
Tiger	Yang Wood	Yang Fire, Yang Earth
Rabbit	Yin Wood	
Dragon	Yang Earth	Yin Wood, Yin Water
Snake	Yang Fire	Yang Earth, Yang Metal
Horse	Yin Fire	Yin Earth
Sheep	Yin Earth	Yin Fire, Yin Wood
Monkey	Yang Metal	Yang Earth, Yang Water
Cock	Yin Metal	
Dog	Yang Earth	Yin Metal, Yin Fire

Chapter 6

Chinese Astrology Calendar

The Chinese Calendar is also called the Natural Energy Calendar or the 10,000 Year Calendar. According to legend it began 2698 B.C.; the first day of the first year of Huang Di, the Yellow Emperor's reign. This calendar is the foundation for Chinese Astrology and most Asian divination systems. The Chinese Astrology Calendar Made Easy ©, incorporates all the necessary elements to calculate an authentic Chinese Astrology Birth Chart. This calendar is used to find the Stem and Branch for any Hour, Day, Month and Year.

The following are four integral components necessary to find correct birth information.

Chinese Age

At birth, a person is considered one year old. When you are 12 years old in the western calendar, you are 13 years old in Chinese Astrology. Add one to the western birth age. This is important for forecasting the timing of events.

Daylight Savings Time

Daylight savings time must be calculated for Tzu Ping astrology. If daylight savings time was used, subtract one hour from your time of birth. This is used to calculate the Four Pillars.

To confirm if daylight savings time was in effect, refer to the following book:

Time Changes in the USA, by Doris Doane.

Place of Birth

Use the time of birth in the city in which you were born. Do not convert to the time in China or any other place.

Solar Calendar

The Chinese Astrology Calendar Made Easy © and Tzu Ping astrology is based on the Solar calendar, not the Lunar calendar.

The following is an example of how to use the Chinese Astrology Calendar Made Easy ©.

Below is year 1931 from the Chinese Astrology Calendar Made Easy ©.

1931

Column 1 ▼	Column 2 ▼		Column 3 ▼		Columns 4	5 ▼	6
	Month		Year				
Find Your Day Here	Stem	Branch	Stem	Branch	Day	Day	Time
January 6–February 5	Yin Earth	Ox	Yang Metal	Horse	Jan	52	15:12
February 5–March 7	Yang Metal	Tiger	Yin Metal	Sheep	Feb	23	2:41
March 7–April 6	Yin Metal	Rabbit	Yin Metal	Sheep	March	51	21:03
April 6–May 7	Yang Water	Dragon	Yin Metal	Sheep	April	22	2:21
May 7–June 7	Yin Water	Snake	Yin Metal	Sheep	May	52	20:10
June 7–July 8	Yang Wood	Horse	Yin Metal	Sheep	June	23	:42
July 8–August 8	Yin Wood	Sheep	Yin Metal	Sheep	July	53	11:06
August 8–September 9	Yang Fire	Monkey	Yin Metal	Sheep	Aug	24	21:20
September 9–October 9	Yin Fire	Cock	Yin Metal	Sheep	Sept	55	:10
October 9–November 8	Yang Earth	Dog	Yin Metal	Sheep	Oct	25	15:33
November 8–December 8	Yin Earth	Pig	Yin Metal	Sheep	Nov	56	17:10
December 8–January 6	Yang Metal	Rat	Yin Metal	Sheep	Dec	26	9:41

Branch	Pig	Rat	Ox	Tiger	Rabbit	Dragon	Snake	Horse	Sheep	Monkey	Cock	Dog
Main Element	Yang Water	Yin Water	Yin Earth	Yang Wood	Yin Wood	Yang Earth	Yang Fire	Yin Fire	Yin Earth	Yang Metal	Yin Metal	Yang Earth
Hidden Elements	Yang Wood		Yin Water	Yang Fire		Yin Wood	Yang Earth	Yin Earth	Yin Fire	Yang Earth		Yin Metal
			Yin Metal	Yang Earth		Yin Water	Yang Metal		Yin Wood	Yang Water		Yin Fire

- Column 1 has solar days. Find the day in question here. This is usually the birthdate, but it can be any day.

- Column 2 is the Stem and Branch for the Month in question. This is the Month Binomial.

- Column 3 is the Year Stem and Branch. This is the Year Binomial.

- Column 4 and 5 are called "Day". These columns are used to find the Day Binomial. Column 4 lists the 12 months. Find the month in question in column 4 and then move to column 5. Column 5 has a special number, this number is used to assist in finding the Day Binomial. Add the day in question to this number. The total creates a binomial number. Find the Binomial number in Table 6, next page.

Table 6

Stem and Branch Cycle of 60

For Hours, Days, Months and Years

Number	1	2	3	4	5	6
Stem	Yang Wood	Yin Wood	Yang Fire	Yin Fire	Yang Earth	Yin Earth
Branch	Rat	Ox	Tiger	Rabbit	Dragon	Snake
Number	7	8	9	10	11	12
Stem	Yang Metal	Yin Metal	Yang Water	Yin Water	Yang Wood	Yin Wood
Branch	Horse	Sheep	Monkey	Cock	Dog	Pig
Number	13	14	15	16	17	18
Stem	Yang Fire	Yin Fire	Yang Earth	Yin Earth	Yang Metal	Yin Metal
Branch	Rat	Ox	Tiger	Rabbit	Dragon	Snake
Number	19	20	21	22	23	24
Stem	Yang Water	Yin Water	Yang Wood	Yin Wood	Yang Fire	Yin Fire
Branch	Horse	Sheep	Monkey	Cock	Dog	Pig
Number	25	26	27	28	29	30
Stem	Yang Earth	Yin Earth	Yang Metal	Yin Metal	Yang Water	Yin Water
Branch	Rat	Ox	Tiger	Rabbit	Dragon	Snake
Number	31	32	33	34	35	36
Stem	Yang Wood	Yin Wood	Yang Fire	Yin Fire	Yang Earth	Yin Earth
Branch	Horse	Sheep	Monkey	Cock	Dog	Pig
Number	37	38	39	40	41	42
Stem	Yang Metal	Yin Metal	Yang Water	Yin Water	Yang Wood	Yin Wood
Branch	Rat	Ox	Tiger	Rabbit	Dragon	Snake
Number	43	44	45	46	47	48
Stem	Yang Fire	Yin Fire	Yang Earth	Yin Earth	Yang Metal	Yin Metal
Branch	Horse	Sheep	Monkey	Cock	Dog	Pig
Number	49	50	51	52	53	54
Stem	Yang Water	Yin Water	Yang Wood	Yin Wood	Yang Fire	Yin Fire
Branch	Rat	Ox	Tiger	Rabbit	Dragon	Snake
Number	55	56	57	58	59	60
Stem	Yang Earth	Yin Earth	Yang Metal	Yin Metal	Yang Water	Yin Water
Branch	Horse	Sheep	Monkey	Cock	Dog	Pig

Branch	Pig	Rat	Ox	Tiger	Rabbit	Dragon	Snake	Horse	Sheep	Monkey	Cock	Dog
Main Element	Yang Water	Yin Water	Yin Earth	Yang Wood	Yin Wood	Yang Earth	Yang Fire	Yin Fire	Yin Earth	Yang Metal	Yin Metal	Yang Earth

Example 1.

February 10, 1931.

Refer to column 4, find February, move to the right and find the number in column 5. The day number is 23. Add 23 to 10 (February 10) which totals 33. "33" is the Binomial for your Day Stem and Branch. Find number 33, in Table 6.

The Day Binomial is Yang Fire, Monkey.

	Hour	Day	Month	Year
Stem		Yang Fire		
Branch		Monkey		

Example 2.

September 20, 1931.

The Day number is 55. Add 20 (September 20) to 55, the total is 75.

Subtract 60 from 75. The binomial is 15 or Yang Earth, Tiger.

* * * * * * * * * *

The binomial chart has 60 segments. If the total of the day in question and day number is greater than 60, subtract 60 from the total. In this case subtract 60 from 75. The result is 15. Find 15 in the Day Stem and Branch Table.

* * * * * * * * * *

	Hour	Day	Month	Year
Stem		Yang Earth		
Branch		Tiger		

• Column 6 is the Month Divider time. If your day is on the first day of the solar month this is the exact time the month changes. This is used for the Month Stem and Branch only.

Chapter 7

Four Pillars

The Four Pillars are Stems and Branches of the Hour, Day, Month and Year of birth. They comprise the constitutional birth chart, which is the foundation for Tzu Ping Chinese Astrology. The Chinese Astrology Calendar Made Easy © is used to obtain the Four Pillars. The following example illustrates how to calculate the Four Pillars. Use the information below or refer to 1931 in the Appendix.

A Male born January 28, 1999 at 5:30 am.

1999

| Find your Day Here | Month | | Year | | Day | Day | Time |
	Stem	Branch	Stem	Branch			
January 6–February 4	Yin Wood	Ox	Yang Earth	Tiger	Jan	49	3 : 00
February 4–March 6	Yang Fire	Tiger	Yin Earth	Rabbit	Feb	20	14 : 42
March 6–April 5	Yin Fire	Rabbit	Yin Earth	Rabbit	March	48	8 : 52
April 5–May 6	Yang Earth	Dragon	Yin Earth	Rabbit	April	19	13 : 55
May 6–June 6	Yin Earth	Snake	Yin Earth	Rabbit	May	49	7 : 29
June 6–July 7	Yang Metal	Horse	Yin Earth	Rabbit	June	20	11 : 51
July 7–August 8	Yin Metal	Sheep	Yin Earth	Rabbit	July	50	22 : 14
August 8–September 8	Yang Water	Monkey	Yin Earth	Rabbit	Aug	21	7 : 57
September 8–October 9	Yin Water	Cock	Yin Earth	Rabbit	Sept	52	11 : 13
October 9–November 7	Yang Wood	Dog	Yin Earth	Rabbit	Oct	22	3 : 06
November 7–December 7	Yin Wood	Pig	Yin Earth	Rabbit	Nov	53	6 : 14
December 7–January 6	Yang Fire	Rat	Yin Earth	Rabbit	Dec	23	21 : 14

1. Find the solar day in column 1.
   Move directly to the right and write down the Month Stem and Branch. Column 2. Yin Wood, Ox. Place this Binomial in the Four Pillar Chart. See below.

	Hour	Day	Month	Year
Stem			Yin Wood	
Branch			Ox	

2. Move directly to the right and write down the Year Stem and Branch. Column 3. Yang Earth, Tiger. See Four Pillars below.

	Hour	Day	Month	Year
Stem			Yin Wood	Yang Earth
Branch			Ox	Tiger

3. Move to the right and find the month in question, January, (column 4) and continue to the right to the Day number, write down the number in the Day Column, Column 5.

   Add the day of birth to this number. 49 plus 28 (January 28)=77.

   77-60=*17*, this is the Day Stem and Branch Binomial.

   As a reminder, the number in this column assists in finding the Binomial for the day of birth. There are 60 Binomials or combinations. If the total of the birthday and the Column Day exceeds 60, subtract 60 from the total. In this example, the total is 77, subtract 60, resulting in Binomial 17.

In the Stem and Branch Cycle of 60 Chart, see next page, find Binomial *17*, this is the Day Stem and Branch Binomial.Yang Metal, Dragon. Place this Binomial in the Four Pillars. See below.

	Hour	Day	Month	Year
Stem		Yang Metal	Yin Wood	Yang Earth
Branch		Dragon	Ox	Tiger

Stem and Branch Cycle of 60

For Hours, Days, Months and Years

Number	1	2	3	4	5	6
Stem	Yang Wood	Yin Wood	Yang Fire	Yin Fire	Yang Earth	Yin Earth
Branch	Rat	Ox	Tiger	Rabbit	Dragon	Snake
Number	7	8	9	10	11	12
Stem	Yang Metal	Yin Metal	Yang Water	Yin Water	Yang Wood	Yin Wood
Branch	Horse	Sheep	Monkey	Cock	Dog	Pig
Number	13	14	15	16	17	18
Stem	Yang Fire	Yin Fire	Yang Earth	Yin Earth	Yang Metal	Yin Metal
Branch	Rat	Ox	Tiger	Rabbit	Dragon	Snake
Number	19	20	21	22	23	24
Stem	Yang Water	Yin Water	Yang Wood	Yin Wood	Yang Fire	Yin Fire
Branch	Horse	Sheep	Monkey	Cock	Dog	Pig
Number	25	26	27	28	29	30
Stem	Yang Earth	Yin Earth	Yang Metal	Yin Metal	Yang Water	Yin Water
Branch	Rat	Ox	Tiger	Rabbit	Dragon	Snake
Number	31	32	33	34	35	36
Stem	Yang Wood	Yin Wood	Yang Fire	Yin Fire	Yang Earth	Yin Earth
Branch	Horse	Sheep	Monkey	Cock	Dog	Pig
Number	37	38	39	40	41	42
Stem	Yang Metal	Yin Metal	Yang Water	Yin Water	Yang Wood	Yin Wood
Branch	Rat	Ox	Tiger	Rabbit	Dragon	Snake
Number	43	44	45	46	47	48
Stem	Yang Fire	Yin Fire	Yang Earth	Yin Earth	Yang Metal	Yin Metal
Branch	Horse	Sheep	Monkey	Cock	Dog	Pig
Number	49	50	51	52	53	54
Stem	Yang Water	Yin Water	Yang Wood	Yin Wood	Yang Fire	Yin Fire
Branch	Rat	Ox	Tiger	Rabbit	Dragon	Snake
Number	55	56	57	58	59	60
Stem	Yang Earth	Yin Earth	Yang Metal	Yin Metal	Yang Water	Yin Water
Branch	Horse	Sheep	Monkey	Cock	Dog	Pig

Branch	Pig	Rat	Ox	Tiger	Rabbit	Dragon	Snake	Horse	Sheep	Monkey	Cock	Dog
Main Element	Yang Water	Yin Water	Yin Earth	Yang Wood	Yin Wood	Yang Earth	Yang Fire	Yin Fire	Yin Earth	Yang Metal	Yin Metal	Yang Earth

4. Refer to the Hour Stem and Branch Chart, find the *Day Stem* in the top row and look directly below it to the Stem and Branch which corresponds to the time of birth.

Day Stem is Yang Metal, move to 5:30 am which is Yin Earth, Rabbit. This is the Hour Stem and Branch. See below.

Hour Stem and Branch Chart

Day Stem ⟶	Yang Wood Yin Earth	Yang Metal Yin Wood	Yang Fire Yin Metal	Yang Water Yin Fire	Yang Earth Yin Water
11 pm-1 am	Yang Wood Rat	Yang Fire Rat	Yang Earth Rat	Yang Metal Rat	Yang Water Rat
1 am-3 am	Yin Wood Ox	Yin Fire Ox	Yin Earth Ox	Yin Metal Ox	Yin Water Ox
3 am-5 am	Yang Fire Tiger	Yang Earth Tiger	Yang Metal Tiger	Yang Water Tiger	Yang Wood Tiger
5 am-7 am	Yin Fire Rabbit	Yin Earth Rabbit	Yin Metal Rabbit	Yin Water Rabbit	Yin Wood Rabbit
7 am-9 am	Yang Earth Dragon	Yang Metal Dragon	Yang Water Dragon	Yang Wood Dragon	Yang Fire Dragon
9 am-11 am	Yin Earth Snake	Yin Metal Snake	Yin Water Snake	Yin Wood Snake	Yin Fire Snake
11 am-1 pm	Yang Metal Horse	Yang Water Horse	Yang Wood Horse	Yang Fire Horse	Yang Earth Horse
1 pm-3 pm	Yin Metal Sheep	Yin Water Sheep	Yin Wood Sheep	Yin Fire Sheep	Yin Earth Sheep
3 pm-5 pm	Yang Water Monkey	Yang Wood Monkey	Yang Fire Monkey	Yang Earth Monkey	Yang Metal Monkey
5 pm-7 pm	Yin Water Cock	Yin Wood Cock	Yin Fire Cock	Yin Earth Cock	Yin Metal Cock
7 pm- 9 pm	Yang Wood Dog	Yang Fire Dog	Yang Earth Dog	Yang Metal Dog	Yang Water Dog
9 pm-11 pm	Yin Wood Pig	Yin Fire Pig	Yin Earth Pig	Yin Metal Pig	Yin Water Pig

The Four Pillars have now been calculated and read as follows:

Four Pillars

	Hour	Day	Month	Year
Stem	Yin Earth	Yang Metal	Yin Wood	Yang Earth
Branch	Rabbit	Dragon	Ox	Tiger

Example

Find the Four Pillars for the following person and confirm your calculations. The following is the step by step process for calculating the Four Pillars.

Male born on June 30, 1957.
6:30 am daylight savings time.

1. Find the Year in question in the Chinese Calendar Made Easy ©, see calendar below.

2. Find the day in question in column 1.

3. Column 2 is the Month Stem and Branch.

4. Column 3 is the Year Stem and Branch.

5. Find the month in question in Column 4, locate the Day number in column 5. Add the day in question to this, the result is the Day Binomial. Refer to the Stem and Branch Cycle of 60 and find the Binomial. This is the Day Stem and Branch.

6. Refer to the Hour Stem and Branch chart, find the Day Stem in the top row and move down until the time of birth. This is the Hour Stem and Branch.

1957

Find your Day Here	Month Stem	Month Branch	Year Stem	Year Branch	Day	Time
January 5–February 4	Yin Metal	Ox	Yang Fire	Monkey	4	22:11
February 4–March 6	Yang Water	Tiger	Yin Fire	Cock	40	9:55
March 6–April 5	Yin Water	Rabbit	Yin Fire	Cock	8	4:11
April 5–May 6	Yang Wood	Dragon	Yin Fire	Cock	39	9:19
May 6–June 6	Yin Wood	Snake	Yin Fire	Cock	9	3:11
June 6–July 7	Yang Fire	Horse	Yin Fire	Cock	40	7:25
July 7–August 8	Yin Fire	Sheep	Yin Fire	Cock	10	17:49
August 8–September 8	Yang Earth	Monkey	Yin Fire	Cock	41	3:33
September 8–October 8	Yin Earth	Cock	Yin Fire	Cock	12	7:03
October 8–November 8	Yang Metal	Dog	Yin Fire	Cock	42	21:31
November 8–December 7	Yin Metal	Pig	Yin Fire	Cock	13	1:37
December 7–January 6	Yang Water	Rat	Yin Fire	Cock	43	17:57

The Four Pillars for this person is:

Four Pillars

	Hour	Day	Month	Year
Stem	Yin Wood	Yin Water	Yang Fire	Yin Fire
Branch	Rabbit	Cock	Horse	Cock
Elements	Yin Wood	Yin Metal	Yin Fire Yin Earth	Yin Metal

Chapter 8

10 Year Luck Cycles

Luck cycles are Stem and Branch influences during 10 Year segments throughout a lifetime. These cycles combine with the Four Pillars. Good Fortune arrives when 10 Year Luck Cycles provide beneficial elements. When unfavorable elements enter a new cycle, Poor Fortune occurs. Ten Year Luck Cycles represent nature's variable or dynamic influences.

Ten Year Luck Cycles are more influential than Day, Month or Yearly cycles. Branches are the foundation, which set the theme for a time period. Stems represent variations from the basic theme of a cycle.

Four Pillars   10 Year Luck Cycles

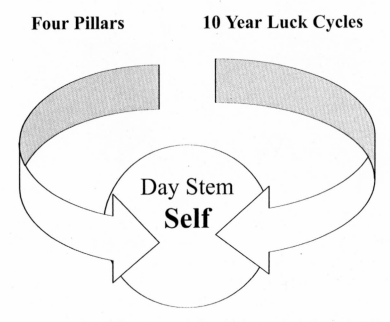

The Self is influenced by all Stems and Branches in the Four Pillars and 10 Year Luck cycles. They both must be evaluated to gain a complete understanding of a person. The major difference between the two is the Four Pillars are constant and the 10 Year Luck Cycles change every ten years, providing dynamic variations of influence throughout a lifetime.

Calculating 10 Year Luck Cycles

1. Determine if the person is Male or Female.
2. Find the polarity of the Year of birth Branch and note whether the main element is Yin or Yang. The following table shows the elements for this calculation.

Branch	Pig	Rat	Ox	Tiger	Rabbit	Dragon	Snake	Horse	Sheep	Monkey	Cock	Dog
Main Element	Yin Water	Yang Water	Yin Earth	Yang Wood	Yin Wood	Yang Earth	Yin Fire	Yang Fire	Yin Earth	Yang Metal	Yin Metal	Yang Earth

For example, Horse is *Yang* Fire or Rabbit is *Yin* Wood.

3. Yin Females count (move) forward in time.
   Yang Females count (move) backward in time.

   Yang Males count (move) forward in time.
   Yin Males count (move) backward in time.

4. Find the Birth Day in column 1 of the Chinese Astrology Calendar Made Easy ©.

5. If the person is a Yin Female or Yang Male, move forward and count the number of days from the *Birthday* to the end of the solar month (column 1). This is moving forward in time. Use the birthday as the first day counted and the last solar day as a marker. *Do not count the last day.* When counting forward the last day is never counted.

6. If the person is a Yang Female or Yin Male, move backward and count the number of days *from the birthday* to the first day of the solar month (column 1), which is backward in time. Use the birthday as the first day counted and *do count* the first day of the solar month. When counting backward the first day of the month is always counted.

For example,March 15, 1940.

1940 is the Dragon-Yang Earth.
The dividers are March 6–April 5.

If this person is Female, she is a Dragon-Yang Earth, Yang Females count backwards from March 15 to March 6, which is 10 days. We do count March 15, the Birthday, and March 6, the first day in the solar month.

If this person is Male, he is a Yang Dragon, Yang Males count forward from March 15 to April 5. Count the birthday, but not April 5.

If the birthday is on the first day of the solar month refer to the last column in the calendar to find the exact time the month changes. If the birthday is before the month time change, the person falls in the preceding month. If it is after the month time, it is in the current month.

***To assist in counting days, refer to the "Counting Days to 10 Year Cycles". The first month is 31 days, 2nd is 30 days, 3rd is 30 days, 4th is 31 days, 5th is 30 and 6th is 28 days. Circle the birthday and the beginning or ending day of the month. Count from the day in question to the beginning or ending day. Be very attentive about the number of days in the month; for example, are there 28, 29, 30 or 31 days in the person's month?

Counting 10 Year Luck Cycles

1	2	3	4	5	6	7	8	9	10	11	12	13	14	15	16	17	18	19	20
21	22	23	24	25	26	27	28	29	30	31	1	2	3	4	5	6	7	8	9
10	11	12	13	14	15	16	17	18	19	20	21	22	23	24	25	26	27	28	29
30	1	2	3	4	5	6	7	8	9	10	11	12	13	14	15	16	17	18	19
20	21	22	23	24	25	26	27	28	29	30	1	2	3	4	5	6	7	8	9
10	11	12	13	14	15	16	17	18	19	20	21	22	23	24	25	26	27	28	29
30	31	1	2	3	4	5	6	7	8	9	10	11	12	13	14	15	16	17	18
19	20	21	22	23	24	25	26	27	28	29	30	1	2	3	4	5	6	7	8
9	10	11	12	13	14	15	16	17	18	19	20	21	22	23	24	25	26	27	28

7. Divide the total number of days counted by 3.
   Ex. 10 days divided by 3=3, with a remainder of 1.

   3 is the number used.

Remainder guidelines

In other situations the remainder is 0 or 2. The guidelines are:

1) If the remainder is 0, use the original number

2) If the remainder is 1, use the original number.

3) If the remainder is 2, round up one number. For example, if the number was 11. Divide 11 by 3 to obtain 3, with a remainder of 2. Round up to 4.

4 becomes the number used.

The reason for this application is:

1. Each day counted represents four months or 33% of one year.
2. Two days represent eight months, or 66% of a year and is rounded up to the next number.

When the percentage of months is greater than 50%, the number is rounded up.

When the number of days counted is two days or less, use the following method:

>If the number of days is 2, the 10 Year Cycles are 1, 11, 21, 31, 41, 51, etc.
>If the number of days is 1, the 10 Year Cycles are 1, 11, 21, 31, 41, 51, etc.
>If born on the first or last solar day, in other words there are 0 days counted,begin the first 10 Year Luck Cycle at birth. For example,0, 10, 20, 30, 40, 50, 60, 70, 80, 90.

The Month pillar is the Stem and Branch influence used for the time period from Birth to the first 10 Year Luck cycle. The Month pillar is the Parent pillar and has the most influence during childhood.

8. Write numbers left to right.
The first 10 Year Luck Cycle begins with the number calculated. In this case 3.

0 3 13 23 33 43 53 63 73 83 93 103

These represent 10 Year Cycles throughout a life.
In this case, 0-3 years old is the Month Stem and Branch in the Four Pillars.

9. Finding the Stem and Branch for 10 Year Luck Cycles.

A *Yin Female* or *Yang Male* moves forward. Refer to the 60 Stem and Branch cycle chart and find the *Birth Month Stem and Branch Binomial*, place this in age 0. Move forward to the next combination and place it in the first 10 Year Cycle. Continue to the next combination and place that combination in the following 10 year cycle. Continue this process for as many cycles as you prefer.

A *Yang Female* and *Yin Male* moves backwards. Refer to the 60 Stem and Branch cycle chart and find the *Birth Month Stem and Branch Binomial,* place it in age 0. Move backward to the preceding combination and place it in the first 10 Year cycle. Continue moving backwards to the next combination and place that combination in the following 10 year cycle. Continue this process for as many cycles as you prefer.

If you do not understand this section, read this chapter again and review all the examples.

Summary

Type	Method of Counting 10 Year Luck cycles
Yin Female or Yang Male	Count forward from the Birthday to the end of the solar month. *Do not* count the last solar day.
Yang Female or Yin Male	Count backwards from the Birthday to the first day of the solar month. *Do* count the first day of the solar month.
	In both cases *do* count the Birthday.

Stem and Branch Cycle of 60

For Hours, Days, Months and Years

Number	1	2	3	4	5	6
Stem	Yang Wood	Yin Wood	Yang Fire	Yin Fire	Yang Earth	Yin Earth
Branch	Rat	Ox	Tiger	Rabbit	Dragon	Snake
Number	7	8	9	10	11	12
Stem	Yang Metal	Yin Metal	Yang Water	Yin Water	Yang Wood	Yin Wood
Branch	Horse	Sheep	Monkey	Cock	Dog	Pig
Number	13	14	15	16	17	18
Stem	Yang Fire	Yin Fire	Yang Earth	Yin Earth	Yang Metal	Yin Metal
Branch	Rat	Ox	Tiger	Rabbit	Dragon	Snake
Number	19	20	21	22	23	24
Stem	Yang Water	Yin Water	Yang Wood	Yin Wood	Yang Fire	Yin Fire
Branch	Horse	Sheep	Monkey	Cock	Dog	Pig
Number	25	26	27	28	29	30
Stem	Yang Earth	Yin Earth	Yang Metal	Yin Metal	Yang Water	Yin Water
Branch	Rat	Ox	Tiger	Rabbit	Dragon	Snake
Number	31	32	33	34	35	36
Stem	Yang Wood	Yin Wood	Yang Fire	Yin Fire	Yang Earth	Yin Earth
Branch	Horse	Sheep	Monkey	Cock	Dog	Pig
Number	37	38	39	40	41	42
Stem	Yang Metal	Yin Metal	Yang Water	Yin Water	Yang Wood	Yin Wood
Branch	Rat	Ox	Tiger	Rabbit	Dragon	Snake
Number	43	44	45	46	47	48
Stem	Yang Fire	Yin Fire	Yang Earth	Yin Earth	Yang Metal	Yin Metal
Branch	Horse	Sheep	Monkey	Cock	Dog	Pig
Number	49	50	51	52	53	54
Stem	Yang Water	Yin Water	Yang Wood	Yin Wood	Yang Fire	Yin Fire
Branch	Rat	Ox	Tiger	Rabbit	Dragon	Snake
Number	55	56	57	58	59	60
Stem	Yang Earth	Yin Earth	Yang Metal	Yin Metal	Yang Water	Yin Water
Branch	Horse	Sheep	Monkey	Cock	Dog	Pig

Branch	Pig	Rat	Ox	Tiger	Rabbit	Dragon	Snake	Horse	Sheep	Monkey	Cock	Dog
Main Element	Yang Water	Yin Water	Yin Earth	Yang Wood	Yin Wood	Yang Earth	Yang Fire	Yin Fire	Yin Earth	Yang Metal	Yin Metal	Yang Earth
Hidden Elements	Yang Wood		Yin Water Yin Metal	Yang Fire Yang Earth		Yin Wood Yin Water	Yang Earth Yang Metal	Yin Earth	Yin Fire Yin Wood	Yang Earth Yang Water		Yin Metal Yin Fire

Example

A male born on June 30, 1957 at 6:30 am daylight savings time.

Four Pillars

	Hour	Day	Month	Year
Stem	Yin Wood	Yin Water	Yang Fire	Yin Fire
Branch	Rabbit	Cock	Horse	Cock
Elements	Yin Wood	Yin Metal	Yin Fire Yin Earth	Yin Metal
	Birth	Aging	Void	Aging

10 Year Luck Cycles

Age	0	8	18	28	38	48	58	68	78
Stem	Yang Fire	Yin Wood	Yang Wood	Yin Water	Yang Water	Yin Metal	Yang Metal	Yin Earth	Yang Earth
Branch	Horse	Snake	Dragon	Rabbit	Tiger	Ox	Rat	Pig	Dog
Main Element	Yin Fire	Yang Fire	Yang Earth	Yin Wood	Yang Wood	Yin Earth	Yin Water	Yang Water	Yang Earth
Hidden Elements	Yin Earth	Yang Earth Yang Metal	Yin Wood Yin Water		Yang Fire Yang Earth	Yin Water Yin Metal		Yang Water Yang Wood	Yin Metal Yin Fire

The birthday is June 30, 1957. This is Yin Cock or Yin Male, count backwards. The solar month is June 6-July 7. Count from June 30 to June 6. Include the first solar day and the birthday. There are 25 days. Divide 25 by 3 to get 8 with a remainder of 1.

Do not round up, use 8. Eight years to 17 years is the first 10 Year Luck Cycle. See example above.

The Month Stem and Branch is Yin Fire/Horse or number 43 in the 60 Stem and Branch Cycle Chart, place this in the 0 time frame. This is a Yin Male, count backward. Place number 42, Yin Wood, Snake in the first 10 Year cycle, which is 8 years old, place number 41 in 18 years old, continue for as many 10 year cycles as you prefer.

Chapter 9

Heavenly Influences

Heavenly Influences reflect a major aspect of one's destiny. They provide information about how a person will live life or reveal their most compatible life path. There are five aspects to this evaluation. Each aspect is based on the Five Element relationship of the Day Stem to the Hour, Day, Month and Year Stems and Branches. The following chart summarizes each type. Additionally, each type is categorized into two parts, which is explained in the Heavenly Influence Table.

Relationship to Day Stem	Type of Relationship	Qualities of Relationships
Sibling Same as Day Stem	Friends	Represents friends, supporters, assistance, and competitors.
Child	Expression	Represents creations, production, manifesting, talent.
Grandchild	Wealth	Represents income, finances, materialism. For males their Spouse.
Grandparent	Power	Represents power, leadership, management, discipline, ambition. For females their spouse.
Parent	Resource	Represents love, nourishment, support.

Calculating Heavenly Influences

1. Find the Day Stem in the top row of the chart below.
2. Move down and locate the Hour Stem in the first column. Write down the number in the box, which intersects the Day Stem and Hour Stem. This is the Heavenly Influence for the Hour Stem to the Day Stem.
3. Repeat this for the Month and Year Stems.
4. Find the Day Stem in the top row, then locate the Five Element for of each of the Branches. Write down the numbers of the Heavenly Influence. Perform this calculation for the Hidden Elements, as well as the main elements for each Branch.
5. Refer to the Heavenly Influences chart on the next page for a description of each Heavenly Influence. These qualities are major contributors towards determining a person's life path and destiny.

Day Stem or Self

Five Element ↓	Yang Wood	Yin Wood	Yang Fire	Yin Fire	Yang Earth	Yin Earth	Yang Metal	Yin Metal	Yang Water	Yin Water
Yang Wood	4	3	2	1	8	7	10	9	5	6
Yin Wood	3	4	1	2	7	8	9	10	6	5
Yang Fire	5	6	4	3	2	1	8	7	10	9
Yin Fire	6	5	3	4	1	2	7	8	9	10
Yang Earth	10	9	5	6	4	3	2	1	8	7
Yin Earth	9	10	6	5	3	4	1	2	7	8
Yang Metal	8	7	10	9	5	6	4	3	2	1
Yin Metal	7	8	9	10	6	5	3	4	1	2
Yang Water	2	1	8	7	10	9	5	6	4	3
Yin Water	1	2	7	8	9	10	6	5	3	4

Heavenly Influences Chart

Relationship	Type	Meaning
Mother Element of Day Stem. Resource	1. Primary Resource Two different genders. Example: *Yin* Water and *Yang* Metal	Primary Resource, represents love, nourishment, support and new opportunities. Support comes from parents, relatives or superiors. If this influence has strong support, they have a high standard in life, the capacity to be a leader and achieve success. If they do not have strong support, they need to prepare to achieve success.
	2. Inconsistent Resource Same gender. Example: *Yang* Water and *Yang* Metal.	Inconsistent Resource, represents inconsistent receiving of support or love during life. They have difficulties in relationships, may lack patience and are susceptible to jealousy. Conditional love is or has been predominant in life. Challenges and obstacles confront them. Focus on overcoming the conditional nature of one's life and success can be achieved.
Same Element as the Day Stem. Sibling	3. Friends-Competitors Opposite genders. Example: *Yang* Water and *Yin* Water	Friends-Competitors, represent help, support or assistance from friends, family or superiors, also, competitors or enemies. Combined with a weak Day Stem, this is more powerful than Friends; it provides strong support. Combined with a strong Day Stem, this creates competitors or enemies
	4. Friends Two of the same sign. Example: *Yang* Water and *Yang* Water	Friends, represents help, support or assistance, from friends, family or superiors.
Offspring of the Day Stem. The child. Expressions	5. Proper Expression Same gender. Example: *Yang* Wood and *Yang* Fire.	Proper Expression, represents creations, productions or achievements. It is showing, displaying, performing or manifesting skills and abilities.
	6. Powerful Expression Opposite genders. Example: *Yang* Wood and *Yin* Fire.	Powerful Expression, represents creations, productions or achievements. It is showing, displaying, performing or manifesting skills and abilities. It is *more* aggressive and powerful than Proper Expression. This force tends to express itself in an abrasive way, lacking sensitivity for others.

Heavenly Influences

Relationship	Type	Meaning
Grandparent is the controller of Day Stem. **Power** For women this represents their Spouse.	7. Proper Power Opposite genders. Example: *Yang* Metal and *Yin* Fire.	Proper Power, represents leadership, control, authority, achievement and level of sophistication. It reflects responsibility, organization, honesty and the ability to use power in a positive way. If it has good support, there is a great chance for success. If little support, there will be many challenges, one needs proper timing to obtain success.
	8. Aggressive Power Same gender. Example: *Yang* Metal and *Yang* Fire.	Aggressive Power, is similar to Proper Power, but emphasizes courage and aggressiveness. It reflects using power to achieve, often it is exerted in an insensitive way; their is a tendency to break rules and pave their own path. If one obtains good support and prepares for opportunities, success will be obtained. If there is a lack of support, many challenges and obstacles will appear. The tendency is to be aggressive or insensitive to others during pressure and stress.
Grandson of the Day Stem. **Wealth** For men this represents their Spouse.	9. Primary Wealth Opposite gender. Example: *Yang* Earth and *Yin* Water.	Primary Wealth, reflects wealth, finances, planning and organization. It reflects good planning and the capacity to develop a good career, with a steady flow of income. If it has strong support, a high level of success comes quickly and smoothly. If weak support, it takes time to build career and wealth.
	10. Dynamic Wealth Same Gender. Example: *Yang* Earth and *Yang* Water.	Dynamic Wealth, is similar to Primary Wealth, the difference is this is more volatile in how wealth is obtained and managed. They obtain wealth, but it is difficult to keep; and they enjoy spending. If this has strong support and a good 10 Year Luck cycle, a great chance to obtain quick wealth and it can be saved. If they have little or no support, money comes and goes.

The following illustrates the procedure to calculate these relationships.

1. Compare the Day Stem to the Hour Stem. Write down the Five Element relationship.

Example 1

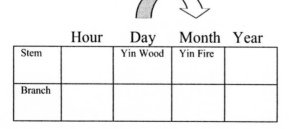

	Hour	Day	Month	Year
Stem	Yang Metal	Yin Water		
Branch				

Hour Stem is Yang Metal, which is the Parent of the Day Stem. This is the Primary Resource relationship, Yang Metal and Yin Water. See Number 1 in the Heavenly Influences chart.

Repeat this process for the Day Stem to Month Stem.
Repeat this process for the Day Stem to Year Stem.

Example 2

	Hour	Day	Month	Year
Stem		Yin Wood	Yin Fire	
Branch				

This is the Expression relationship, Proper Expressions, Yin Wood to Yin Fire (number 5 in the chart). Fire is the Child of Wood.

Example 3

	Hour	Day	Month	Year
Stem	Yang Metal Primary Resource	Yin Water	Yang Earth Proper Power	Yang Fire Primary Wealth
Branch	Dog	Snake	Horse	Cock
Elements	Yang Earth Proper Power	Yang Fire Dynamic Wealth	Yin Fire Dynamic Wealth	Yin Metal Inconsistent Resource
Hidden Elements	Yin Metal Inconsistent Resource	Yang Earth Proper Power	Yin Earth Aggressive Power	
	Yin Fire Dynamic Wealth	Yang Metal Primary Resource		

➤ The Hour Stem is Yang Metal, which is the Parent of the Day Stem, Yin Water. It is Yang Metal to Yin Water, which is Primary Resource. Number 1 in the Heavenly Influence chart.

➤ The Month Stem is Yang Earth, which is the grandparent of the Day Stem, Yin Water. This is Yang to Yin, making it Proper Power or number 7 in the Heavenly Influence chart.

➤ The Year Stem is Yang Fire, which is the Grandchild of the Day Stem, Yin Water. This is Yin to Yang, which is Primary Wealth or number 9 in the Heavenly Influence chart.

➤ The Hour Branch is Dog. The main element is Yang Earth. Yang Earth is the Grandparent of the Day Stem. It is also Yang to Yin making it Proper Power.

One Hidden element is Yin Metal. This is the Mother of the Day Stem element. It is Yin to Yin or Inconsistent Resource.

Another Hidden branch is Yin Fire, which is the Grandchild of the Day Stem. This is Yin to Yin or Dynamic Wealth.

➤The Day Branch is Snake. The main element is Yang Fire, which is the Grandchild of the Day Stem. It is Yang to Yin or Primary Wealth.

One Hidden element is Yang Earth or the Grandparent of the Day Stem. This is Proper Power, Yang to Yin.

The other Hidden element is Yang Metal or Primary Resource.

➤The Month Branch is Horse (Yin Fire). This is the grand-child of the Day Stem or Dynamic wealth.

The Hidden element is Yin Earth, the Grandparent or Aggressive Power.

➤The Year Branch is Cock or Yin Metal. This is Inconsistent Resource.

Example

A male born on June 30, 1957 at 6:30 am daylight savings time.

Four Pillars

	Hour	Day	Month	Year
Stem	Yin Wood Proper Expressions	Yin Water	Yang Fire Primary Wealth	Yin Fire Dynamic wealth
Branch	Rabbit	Cock	Horse	Cock
Elements	Yin Wood Proper Expressions	Yin Metal Inconsistent Resource	Yin Fire Dynamic Wealth	Yin Metal Inconsistent Resource
			Yin Earth Aggressive Power	

Heavenly Influence analysis:

Two Proper Expressions (Child of Day Stem)
Proper Expression, represents creations, productions or achievements. It is showing, displaying, performing or manifesting skills and abilities.

One Primary Wealth and Two Dynamic Wealth.
Primary Wealth reflects wealth, finances, planning and organization. They have a good plan for life and the capacity to develop a good career and a steady flow of income. If they have strong support, a high level of success comes quickly and smoothly. If weak support it takes time to build career and wealth.

Dynamic Wealth represents money coming and going. They obtain money but it is difficult to keep. They enjoy spending. If they have strong support and a good luck cycle, a great chance for quick money and it can be saved. If they have little or no support, money comes and goes.

This person has a mixture of Primary Wealth and Dynamic Wealth. Wealth will be created in numerous ways; they may have periods of steady income and times of variable income. The Month Branch is the Horse or Yin Fire, it is the most influential aspect of the Four Pillars on the Day Stem. The Wealth aspect of life will create many opportunities. If the Cycle provides a weak Day Stem, Wealth will create great pressure. If the Day Stem or Self is strong, there are many opportunities to build Wealth. Timing will be crucial for this person.

Wealth or Fire has strong Support in the Hour Pillar, because the two woods make Fire stronger. The Horse-Fire in the Month, provides Root to the Fire in the Month and Year Stems, making Wealth the Predominant Heavenly Influence.

One Aggressive Power

They use power to achieve things even when not necessary. The power is often exerted in an abrasive way, they want people to follow them and have a tendency to break rules and pave their own path.

If they obtain support and prepare for opportunities they can obtain success. If there is little support, many challenges and obstacles will appear. The tendency is to be aggressive or manipulate others during pressure and stress.

This is a deceiving Influence. It is a Hidden Element in the Month Branch, it has strong support from the three Fires in the Chart. This person has the capacity to lead and exert influence over others. He must be careful not to allow the edginess or abrasiveness to dominate his actions. The best success will occur during times when the Self is strong. This allows him to have the strength to handle pressure in a gentle way. If the Self is weak, the pressure will allow edginess to be easily expressed.

Two Inconsistent Resource

They receive or give mixed types of support in their life. Difficulties in relationships, may lack patience and are susceptible to jealousy. Conditional love has been a major issue in their life. Challenges and obstacles confront them. They need to focus on overcoming the conditional nature of life, then success can be achieved.

The Cock or Inconsistent Resource, which is the Day and Year Branches, provides nourishment to the Day Stem. The Day Branch is close to the Day Stem and provides direct support. The Year Yin Metal or Cock, is Blocked by the Month Pillar, which is all Fire. This much needed Metal, cannot get to the Day Stem directly. When the Day Stem is in a weak period this aspect of life will become predominant. He needs to focus on developing nurturing and unconditional relationships to feel complete and fulfilled.

Predominant Heavenly Influence

There are a variety of Heavenly Influences in each Four Pillar chart; identifying the predominant Heavenly Influence will reveal a life path. The procedure is a four step process.

1. Identify the main Element in the Month Branch. If this element is also found in the Hour, Month or Year Stem, but not in the Day Stem, this Element is the predominant

Element. The Heavenly Influence it has with the Day Stem, is the predominant influence.

2. If the main element of the Month Branch is not in the Stems, look to the Hidden Elements. If the *first* Hidden Element is found in the Stems, but not the Day Stem, that element and its Heavenly Influence with the Day Stem, is the predominant influence in the chart.

3. If the main element and first hidden element are not in the Stems, and there is a second hidden element, refer to it. If the second Hidden Element is found in the Stems, but not the Day Stem, this is the predominant Heavenly Influence.

4. If the main or Hidden Elements are not in the Stems, use the main element of the Branch as the predominant element, and its relationship with the day Stem, as the predominant Heavenly Influence.

Example

A male born on June 30, 1957 at 6:30 am daylight savings time.

Four Pillars

	Hour	Day	Month	Year
Stem	Yin Wood Proper Expressions	Yin Water	Yang Fire Primary Wealth	Yin Fire Dynamic wealth
Branch	Rabbit	Cock	Horse	Cock
Elements	Yin Wood Proper Expressions	Yin Metal Inconsistent Resource	Yin Fire Dynamic Wealth Yin Earth Aggressive Power	Yin Metal Inconsistent Resource

The main element in the Month Branch is Fire. Fire is in the Month and Year Stems, making Dynamic Wealth the predominant influence.

Chapter 10

Stem Transformations

One of the underlying principles in Astrology is change. The Five Element quality of Stems and Branches change with specific combinations. It is like mixing colors together. Certain colors combine to create a new color. When certain elements mix, they convert into a new, single element. The transformation occurs under specific conditions.

Transformations can occur in the Four Pillars, 10 Year Luck Cycles, Yearly or Monthly time frames. If the transformation occurs in the Four Pillars, the change exists for a lifetime. If an element, from a future cycle of time, combines with an element from the Four Pillars, the transformation lasts for the duration of the cycle of time. When the time frame ends, the transformed element reverts back to its original element. For example, it takes two stems to cause a transformation, if one is in the Four Pillars and one appears in a particular year, the transformation occurs for that year. After the year, the new element reverts back to the original element.

Good fortune, is when a new transformed element benefits the Self.

Bad fortune, is when a new transformed element hinders the Self.

The following are Stem transformations.

Stem Combinations	Transforms into this New Element
Yang Wood and Yin Earth	Earth
Yang Metal and Yin Wood	Metal
Yang Fire and Yin Metal	Water
Yang Water and Yin Fire	Wood
Yang Earth and Yin Water	Fire

Each transformation includes the controlling Five Element relationship. For example, Wood controls Earth and Metal controls Wood. The controlling element is always Yang (Yang Wood) and the element controlled is always Yin (Yin Earth).

Yang Fire combines with Yin Metal. See example 1a.

Example 1a

	Hour	Day	Month	Year
Stem	Yang Water	Yin Water	*Yang Fire*	*Yin Metal*
Branch				

Yang Fire and Yin Metal transform into Water. View them both as Water. See example 1b.

Example 1b

	Hour	Day	Month	Year
Stem	Yang Water	Yin Water	*Water*	*Water*
Branch				

Yang Wood and Yin Earth transform into Earth, view both as Earth, see examples 2a and 2b.

Example 2a.

	Hour	Day	Month	Year
Stem	Yin Earth	Yin Metal	*Yang Wood*	*Yin Earth*
Branch				

Example 2b

	Hour	Day	Month	Year
Stem	Yin Earth	Yin Metal	*Earth*	*Earth*
Branch				

Transformation Rules

Transformations occur under specific conditions. The following are the conditions and *all* conditions must exist.

1. Stems combine only when they are next to each other. See examples 1 and 2. In those examples, the Month and Year Stems transform. If the Four Pillar chart was Example 3, The Hour stem and Year Stem would not transform, they are not adjacent.

Example 3

	Hour	Day	Month	Year
Stem	*Yang Wood*	Yin Metal	Yang Water	*Yin Earth*
Branch				

2. If the Month and Year Stems have a transformation combination, find which element would be the new element. Look at the Month Branch, if the Month Branch provides root, which means it is the same element as the new transformed element, then the transformation will occur. This root can be in the main or Hidden elements. Refer to example 4a and 4b.

3. When a Stem trasforms, the new element takes the polarity of the main element of the Month branch. This is used to determine the type of Heavenly Influence.

Example 4a.

Four Pillars

	Hour	Day	Month	Year
Stem	Yin Wood	Yin Water	Yang Fire	Yin Metal
Branch	Rabbit	Cock	Pig	Cock
Elements	Yin Wood	Yin Metal	Yang Water Yang Wood	Yin Metal

Example 4b.

Transforms to this Chart

	Hour	Day	Month	Year
Stem	Yin Wood	Yin Water	Water	Water
Branch	Rabbit	Cock	Pig	Cock
Elements	Yin Wood	Yin Metal	Yang Water Yang Wood	Yin Metal

In 4a, the Yang Fire in the Month Stem combines with the Yin Metal in the Year Stem, transforming to Water. For the transformation to occur, the Month Branch must provide root. The Month Branch is Pig, which contains Yang Water and Yang Wood. The Yang Water provides a Main root, because it is the main element of the Pig. This root is the catalyst for the transformation, it allows it to occur. Example 4b, reflects the new transformed element.

Day Master Transformations

The Day Stem requires special conditions for a transformation. All conditions must exist for a Day Stem transformation. The following are the conditions.

1. The Day Stem combines only with the Hour Stem or Month Stem, the adjacent Pillars.

2. The new element formed by the transformation must have root in the Month Branch.

3. If the Day Stem element is also in the Hour, Month or Year Stems, there *cannot* be a transformation.

4. There cannot be a grandparent element of the new Transformed Element, anywhere in the Four Pillars. This includes Stems, Main or Hidden elements.

5. The new Transformed element must have its Parent element in the Four Pillars.

The following table summarizes each of the Day Stem transformations.

Day Stem Transformations

	New Element	Month Branch (Must be present)	Controlling Element *(Cannot have)*
Yang Metal & Yin Wood	Metal	Ox, Snake Cock or Monkey	Fire not as a main element.
Yang Wood & Yin Earth	Earth	Ox, Dragon, Sheep or Dog	Wood not as a main element.
Yang Fire & Yin Metal	Water	Rat, Dragon, Monkey or Pig	No Earth in Stems. No Sheep or Dog.
Yang Water & Yin Fire	Wood	Tiger, Rabbit, Sheep or Pig	Metal not as a main element.
Yang Earth & Yin Water	Fire	Tiger, Snake, Horse or Dog	Water not as a main element.

Chapter 11

Day Stem or Self

The Day Stem is considered the centerpiece of the Four Pillars; it reflects the "Self". Some astrologers refer to this as the *Day Master*. How other Stems, Branches and cycles of time affect the Self, is the major focus of Chinese Astrology. In Chinese Astrology, we refer to the condition of the Self Element, it can be very strong, balanced, weak or very weak; this condition is determined by the total mix of elements in the birth chart.

The strength or weakness of the Self is not a definitive cause for success. If the Four Pillars and cycles of time do not give support for success, it means one will have to make his or her own success, one cannot rely on luck or significant support. In this scenario, "Tzu Ping" astrology can identify the probable types of support or challenges and obstacles. Success will follow skilled and informed actions.

Determining Condition of Self

Calculating the condition of the Day Stem is an art and science. The following is a quantitative method for calculating the strength of the Self. In a short period of time, you will be able to calculate the condition of the Day Master by understanding the Five Element relationships of the Four Pillars. The following explains this procedure, and examples follow illustrating this process.

Determining the condition of the Day Master.

1. Allocate the value of 100 to each of the Stems in the Four Pillars. *Do not* include the Day Stem.

2. In Table X, locate the Element value in each of the Branches of the Four Pillars. Include the Hidden Elements.

3. Determine the 12 Stage Growth Cycle for each Element. Table Y contains percentage strengths for each stage. The introduction to Table Y explains this procedure.

4. Multiply the element values found in step 2, by the percentages found in step 3. This is the strength of each element.

5. Determine the Parent and Sibling elements of the Day Stem; total the values of these elements, they are the *Strengthening* factors.

6. Determine the Grandparent, Child and Grandchild elements of the Day Stem; total the values, they are the *Weakening* factors.

7. Compare the two factors. If the Strengthening factors exceed the Weakening factors, the Self is Strong. If the Weakening factors exceed the Strengthening factors, the Self is weak.

Hidden Elements

Nine of the 12 Branches or Animals contain "Hidden Elements". These are minor elements inside a Branch. The Hidden Elements influence each person and must be evaluated. The Hidden Element chart shows the influence or strength of the main and Hidden Elements. The bottom of each page in the Chinese Astrology Calendar Made Easy, contains a box showing the main and Hidden Elements for each Animal.

Table X

Hidden Elements
(Relative Weights)

Animal	Main Element	Hidden Element
Pig	Yang Water 70	Yang Wood 30
Rat	Yin Water 100	
Ox	Yin Earth 60	Yin Water 20, Yin Metal 20
Tiger	Yang Wood 60	Yang Fire 20, Yang Earth 20
Rabbit	Yin Wood 100	
Dragon	Yang Earth 60	Yin Wood 20, Yin Water 20
Snake	Yang Fire 60	Yang Earth 20, Yang Metal 20
Horse	Yin Fire 70	Yin Earth 30
Sheep	Yin Earth 60	Yin Fire 20, Yin Wood 20
Monkey	Yang Metal 60	Yang Earth 20, Yang Water 20
Cock	Yin Metal 100	
Dog	Yang Earth 60	Yin Metal 20, Yin Fire 20

Table Y

12 Stage Growth Cycle

The Day Stem is influenced by all Stems and Branches in the Four Pillars; but the Month Branch has the greatest single influence. The 12 Stage Growth cycle is a more detailed variation of the Yin-Yang and Five Element cycles of expansion, peaking, decline and regeneration. In this analysis each element in the Four Pillars is compared to the element and energy of the Month Branch. The Month Branch reflects the Season of birth. Each element represents a season and each season may nourish, support, weaken or control another element. In this calculation, each of the elements in the Four Pillars is compared to the Month Branch; this determines the influence the Month Branch has on every element in the Four Pillars. The following table shows each element and their corresponding season.

Element	Season
Wood	Spring
Fire	Summer
Earth	Indian Summer
Metal	Fall
Water	Winter

Table X, contains standard values for the elements within Branches, the 12 Stage Growth Cycle determines the actual degree of strength for those standard values.

How to use this table.

1. In the top row, locate each Element in the Four Pillars.

2. Locate the Month Branch from the Four Pillars in the column directly beneath each element. The intersection box of the Element and Month Branch contains the percentage or strength of the 12 Stage Growth Cycle. Take this percentage and multiply it by the Relative weights found in Table X. This total is the strength of each element.

12 Stage Growth Cycle

Element▼ Element▼ Element▼ Element▼

Cycle Stage		Wood	Fire	Earth	Metal	Water
1	Birth	Pig 80 %	Tiger 80 %	Tiger 50%	Snake 80%	Monkey 80%
2	Childhood	Rat 50%	Rabbit 50%	Rabbit 50%	Horse 50%	Cock 50%
3	Adolescence	Ox 50 %	Dragon 50%	Dragon 100%	Sheep 50%	Dog 50%
4	Adulthood	Tiger 100%	Snake 100%	Snake 50%	Monkey 100%	Pig 100%
5	Prime	Rabbit 100%	Horse 100%	Horse 50%	Cock 100%	Rat 100%
6	Decline	Dragon 80%	Sheep 80%	Sheep 100%	Dog 80%	Ox 80%
7	Aging	Snake 50%	Monkey 50%	Monkey 50%	Pig 50%	Tiger 50%
8	Death	Horse 50%	Cock 50%	Cock 50%	Rat 50%	Rabbit 50%
9	Dormancy	Sheep 80%	Dog 80%	Dog 100%	Ox 80%	Dragon 80%
10	Void	Monkey 50%	Pig 50%	Pig 50%	Tiger 50%	Snake 50%
11	Embryo	Cock 50%	Rat 50%	Rat 50%	Rabbit 50%	Horse 50%
12	Pregnancy	Dog 50%	Ox 50%	Ox 100%	Dragon 50%	Sheep 50%

▲ ▲ ▲

Find Month Branch Here

Example

Yin Water Day Master
Male born on June 30, 1957 at 6:30 am daylight savings time.

Four Pillars

	Hour	Day	Month	Year
Stem	Yin Wood Offspring 100 X 50%	Yin Water	Yang Fire Grandchild 100 X 100%	Yin Fire Grandchild 100 X 100%
Branch Elements	Rabbit Yin Wood Offspring 100 X 50%	Cock Yin Metal Parent 100 X 50%	Horse Yin Fire Grandchild 70 X 100% Yin Earth Grandparent 30 X 50%	Cock Yin Metal Parent 100 X 50%

Strengthening Elements:

Resource-Parent: Two Cock Branches: 100+100=200 X 50%=100

Total   Strenghtening Factor   *100*

Weakening Elements:

Expression-Child: Hour Stem & Hour Branch:	200 X 50%=100
Wealth-Grandchild: Month Stem	100 X 100%=100
Year Stem	100 X 100%=100
Month Branch	70 X 100%= 70
Grandparent: Month Hidden Element Branch 30 X 50%=	15

Total   Weakening Factor   *385*

The Strengthening factor is 100 and Weakening is 385.
This is a weak Yin Water Day Master.

Beneficial elements are Water and Metal.
Detrimental elements Earth, Fire, Wood.

12 Stage Growth Cycle

The 12 Stage Growth Cycle is a tool to evaluate the condition of the Self. There are numerous applications of this cycle. The first application was determining the strength of each of the elements in the Four Pillars. A second application identifies personality, traits, emotional conditions, preferences, and compatible professions. This evaluation compares the Day Stem element to the Month Branch. Below is the 12 Stage Growth Cycle Table, followed by detailed information on each cycle.

How to use this chart.

1. Find the Day Stem in the top row.

2. Find the Month Branch (Animal) in the column directly underneath the Day Stem column at the top. The Growth Cycle to the left is your Stage.
   Refer to the detailed 12 Stage Growth Cycle Table.

Day Stem ▼ / Day Stem ▼ / Day Stem ▼ / Day Stem ▼

Cycle Stage	Yang Wood	Yin Wood	Yang Fire	Yin Fire	Yang Earth	Yin Earth	Yang Metal	Yin Metal	Yang Water	Yin Water
Birth	Pig	Horse	Tiger	Cock	Tiger	Cock	Snake	Rat	Monkey	Rabbit
Childhood	Rat	Snake	Rabbit	Monkey	Rabbit	Monkey	Horse	Pig	Cock	Tiger
Adolescence	Ox	Dragon	Dragon	Sheep	Dragon	Sheep	Sheep	Dog	Dog	Ox
Adulthood	Tiger	Rabbit	Snake	Horse	Snake	Horse	Monkey	Cock	Pig	Rat
Prime	Rabbit	Tiger	Horse	Snake	Horse	Snake	Cock	Monkey	Rat	Pig
Decline	Dragon	Ox	Sheep	Dragon	Sheep	Dragon	Dog	Sheep	Ox	Dog
Aging	Snake	Rat	Monkey	Rabbit	Monkey	Rabbit	Pig	Horse	Tiger	Cock
Death	Horse	Pig	Cock	Tiger	Cock	Tiger	Rat	Snake	Rabbit	Monkey
Dormancy	Sheep	Dog	Dog	Ox	Dog	Ox	Ox	Dragon	Dragon	Sheep
Void	Monkey	Cock	Pig	Rat	Pig	Rat	Tiger	Rabbit	Snake	Horse
Embryo	Cock	Monkey	Rat	Pig	Rat	Pig	Rabbit	Tiger	Horse	Snake
Pregnancy	Dog	Sheep	Ox	Dog	Ox	Dog	Dragon	Ox	Sheep	Dragon

Branches ▲ / Branches ▲ / Branches ▲ / Branches ▲

The 12 Stage Growth Cycle

Stage	Name	Personality, traits and compatible professions.
1	Birth Strong Force	Happiness, honesty, kindness, gentleness, good relationships, others like and respect them. A quick learner who is intelligent, lives a long life, and has many opportunities. *Compatible Profession:* Helping or assisting others.
2	Childhood Medium Force	Gradual growth and enjoys new activities. Easily influenced by others and needs inspiration to develop or mature. *Compatible Profession:* Requires stable partners in business and personal relationships.
3	Adolescence Strong Force	Learning to be an adult, developing, maturing, desires fame and leadership. Uses intelligence to succeed. Preparing for success. *Compatible Profession:* Utilizes intelligence and verbal skills. For example; lawyer, accountant, teacher, sales, businessperson.
4	Adulthood Strong Force	Desires fame, management and leadership. Intelligent, mature, honest and open-minded. Is an independent, self-made person. Potential for great wealth, success and fame. *Compatible Profession:* Business owner, executive, leadership or management.
5	Prime Strong Force	Desires fame, ownership and leadership. Great probability for wealth and success. Can be overconfident and questions everything. Adventurous in a dangerous way; does not give up whether right or wrong. This is the peak, should be cautious of decline and loss. Needs a good life plan in order to retain achievements and resources. *Compatible Profession:* Best to own and work at own company. eg. The owner and cook of a restaurant
6	Decline Weak Force	Situation has reached the top and now turns. A nice person, patient, not a big planner. Needs a calm, steady life. Is passive and doesn't challenge authority. Must be steady and consistent to accomplish goals. *Compatible Profession:* A steady, 9-5 job. Find a position where responsibilities end when the work day is completed.

Personality, traits and compatible professions.

		Personality, traits and compatible professions.
7	**Aging** Weak Force	Is the Decline stage but more intense. *Compatible Profession:* Gentle and peaceful work which is not high-pressured.
8	**Death** Weak Force	Hastiness, a chronic worrier, creates a lot of problems and challenges in relationships. Preferable to marry later in life. Needs energy to achieve, as well as exercise and good nutrition to maintain health. *Compatible Profession:* Arts or Literature. Not business management.
9	**Dormancy** Medium Force	Likes to collect things, saves money well, introverted and enjoys indoors. Is cautious, quiet and honest. Needs to be motivated to open up, then can achieve and be successful. Can be very lucky with money if open-minded. *Compatible Profession:* No particular profession is more suitable than another. Must open mind and attitudes to succeed.
10	**Void** Weak Force	Emptiness, worry, impatience, hastiness and doesn't finish things. A poor planner who can be susceptible to being cheated by others. Focus on being calm, careful and serious or many problems and obstacles will surface. Needs support for achievement. *Compatible Profession:* Regular career worker.
11	**Embryo** Medium Force	New beginning. Interested in all things new. Possess a good sense of humor and enjoys helping people. Good luck surrounds him or her. Health is weak when young, but as they age, their health gets better. Likes to know details and reasons for things. Is optimistic about the future. *Compatible Profession:* A helper or assistant, especially in the arts.
12	**Pregnancy** Medium Force	Needs a lot of energy and strong support from family, friends and environment. If he or she perseveres and works hard, they can be successful in career and family. They are honest and social people who are satisfied with their existing lifestyle.

Compatible Profession:
Sales, owner or leadership position.

Example

A male born on June 30, 1957 at 6:30 am daylight savings time.

Four Pillars

	Hour	Day	Month	Year
Stem	Yin Wood	Yin Water	Yang Fire	Yin Fire
Branch	Rabbit	Cock	Horse	Cock
Elements	Yin Wood	Yin Metal	Yin Fire Yin Earth	Yin Metal

Void

12 Stage Growth Cycle

The Day Stem to the Month Branch depicts the Void Stage.

Emptiness, worry, impatience, hastiness and doesn't finish things. A poor planner who can be susceptible to being cheated by others. Focus on being calm, careful and serious or many problems and obstacles will surface. Needs support for achievement.

Compatible Profession:
Regular career worker.

Chapter 12

Five Element Personalities

The following section includes general attributes for each of the Five Elements. A Four Pillar chart contains a blend of Five Elements, the key is learning how to determine the condition of the Self, this will indicate how specific qualities will be expressed. For example, Fire represents charisma, energy and leadership. A weak Fire person, under great stress from their controlling element, may express their Fire nature with frustration, impulsiveness and aggression. The qualities of each element relate directly to the Day Stem. Refer to a person's Day Stem element in this section to obtain additional information about a person. Often a chart will have predominant elements which are not the same as the Day Stem, refer to those elements for additional information about a person.

Water

Water can nourish or deteriorate. Water people communicate well, are gentle, caring and are susceptible to fear. They are not straightforward; they prefer a soft, gentle and indirect way of interaction. Water people are good at both sides of communication, listening and talking. They can use their emotional sensitivity to influence people, but can be greatly influenced by others and their environment. Water people unify others with emotional energy and understanding. They trust their intuition, and use flexibility and perseverance to succeed.

Element	Water
Movement	Adaptable, Flexible
Season	Winter
Direction	North
Planet	Mercury
Color	Blue, Black
Compatible Profession	Teaching, communication, transportation, fishing, divination, lecturing, healers.
Relationships	Water is the sibling. Wood is the child. Fire is the grandchild. Earth is the grandparent. Metal is the parent.

Wood

Wood represents growth. It is expansive and provides direction to achieving goals. Wood people can turn resources into products, ideas into profits, and believe expansion or growth will resolve any problems. Wood people are very sociable and are almost always surrounded by others; they have good verbal skills. Woods are extroverted and love to accomplish or complete activities.

Wood people can have strong tempers and feel frustrated when other people fail to perform to their standards. They can be scattered, spreading themselves and their resources too thin. Wood types may find it difficult to express their inner emotions, have few close friends and can suffer from feeling inadequate. They can handle great amounts of pressure. Wood types are practical people who are always looking to the future.

Element	Wood
Movement	Growth, Ascension.
Season	Spring
Direction	East
Planet	Jupiter
Color	Green
Compatible Profession	Education, writing, publishing, apparel manufacturing, fashion, herbal products, wood related industries.
Relationships	Water is parent. Wood is sibling. Fire is child. Earth is grandchild. Metal is grandparent.

Fire

Fire warms, clarifies and comforts, but can also burn and destroy. It can illuminate or bring light to a situation, or can create explosive actions. Fire people are leaders, motivators and take-charge people. They are highly charismatic, very self-driven, and passionate. If nothing is going on, they will ignite a spark to create something. They are adventurous and are always looking for something new. Change is a predominant theme for them, and they often leap before looking. This can create great successes and great problems. Fire people want to be the center of attention.

Fire people are good speakers, but can be poor listeners. They are creators, and think and act fast. They are brave, take on all challenges, and are good warriors. Fire people can be flamboyant, filled with passion, and make life exciting. They need to keep their excitement, passion and enthusiasm in balance and develop patience.

Element	Fire
Movement	Active, vitality.
Season	Summer
Direction	South
Planet	Mars
Color	Red
Compatible Profession	Restaurant, alcohol, electricity, entertainment, power sources.
Relationships	Wood is the parent. Fire is sibling. Earth is the child. Metal is the grandchild. Water is the grandparent.

Earth

Earth provides stability and is a transformer. In the Five Elements, it is the transforming energy from one season to another or from one element to another. Fairness is often a predominant quality in an Earth person and they tend to be chronic worriers, in fact they may worry about everything, not only their direct life, but everything in the universe. They are steady and do not move as fast as others, but what they lack in speed, they make up with consistency and longevity. They do not like to waste their time in grand schemes or ideas; instead, they plow through the realities of a situation.

Earth people make wonderful managers or organizers, they can be trusted with implementing a plan. However, their focus, practicality and perseverance may result in a single-mindeness which hinders versatility and the ability to handle multiple factors simultaneously. Earth people are not overly emotional, but are sensitive. They resolve emotional problems in practical, concrete ways. Earth people expect the rest of the world to view life as they do, if they do not, Earth types can become stubborn and rigid. They respond well to change, if the change is slow and gradual, abrupt changes disturb them.

Element	Earth
Movement	Stability, stillness.
Season	Indian Summer.
Direction	North East, South West, Center
Planet	Saturn
Color	Yellow, beige.
Compatible Profession	Construction, real estate, attorney, judges, human resources, management, consultation.
Relationships	Fire is the parent. Earth is the sibling. Metal is the child. Water is the grandchild. Wood is the grandparent.

Metal

Metal can be a precious substance, for example, Gold, or a destructive device, a sword. Metal communicates information, it can relay information smoothly. Metal people can gather others for positive goals or negative objectives. They can be focused, emotional, intuitive, confident and aggressive in pursuing goals. Metals tend to be loners, isolated and often withdraw. Metal types may be stubborn, driven by an inner faith whether they are right or wrong. They can be extremely driven to pursue their goals. When problems arise, they will turn inward to find answers, and cannot be expected to communicate their inner feelings. Metals can be successful in any profession, and can also motivate others to achieve common objectives.

Metals can be susceptible to sadness, which can dominate their life. If they become more flexible and open, they will develop loyal friendships. Metal represents righteousness, justice and truth, as well as, sadness, grief, and longing.

Element	Metal
Movement	Inward
Season	Fall
Direction	West, North West
Planet	Venus
Color	White, Gold
Compatible Profession	Metal related industries, strategic management, automobile industry, and jewelry.
Relationships	Water is the child. Wood is the grandchild. Fire is the grandparent. Earth is the parent. Metal is the sibling.

Chapter 13

Five Element Interactions

The Five Elements have a variety of effects in Chinese Astrology. The following section includes a variety of Five Element relationships related to the Day Master.

1. Expressions are the Child relationship to the Day Stem. Expressions or offspring reduce the Day Stem and control Power or the grandparent element of the Day Stem. See diagram below. Expressions can reduce positive or negative Power Influences. If Expression is needed for a person to produce, and its energy is used to control an excess Power, the person may feel very frustrated due to the inability to produce or create. The energy is used to protect the Day Stem from excess Power, instead of being productive.

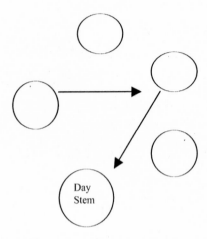

2. Wealth or grandchild is parent to Power. Wealth also controls Resource or parent of the Day Stem. See below. Wealth can produce additional Power, if there is too much Power, it will become even stronger and dominate Day Master. Wealth is also the controlling element of Resource. If Resource is weak and Wealth is excess, Wealth will further weaken the Day Stem by controlling is parent, the person will be weak and deficient. If the Day Master is too strong and has a lot of Resource, strong Wealth will control the Resource. Too much Resource with a strong Day Stem may cause someone to be very spoiled.

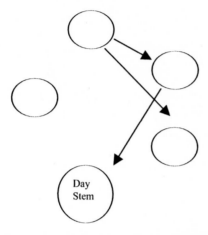

3. Power is parent to the Resource of the Day Master. See below. Power controls Day Stem and also nourishes the parent of the Day Master.

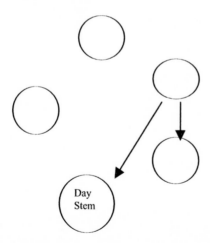

4. Resource nourishes Day Master and controls Expressions, the child of Day Stem.

See below.

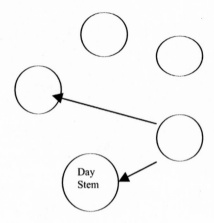

Chapter 14

Stem and Branch Interactions

Stems and Branches reflect the energy of nature and how those energies influence individuals. The interactions create the probability for specific qualities or activities to occur. Depending on the condition of the Self and specific Stem and Branch interactions, a positive or negative influence appears. This principle is true for all interactions in Tzu Ping Astrology. Often you will find seemingly contradictory activities occurring. This is a normal part of life. Financial success can be accompanied with health or relationship difficulties. These are normal occurrences in life and they must appear in Tzu Ping Astrology. It increases the richness and depth of this ancient system.

This section has two major applications. The first is evaluating interactions in the Four Pillars, especially, Clashes, Push Out, Conflict, Trinity and Six Combinations. Those interactions contribute towards determining the strength of the Day Master. The second includes additional information about personality characteristics and traits. Once the condition of the Self is determined evaluate the interactions between the Stems and Branches in the Four Pillars and cycles of time.

Stems and Branches reflect influences of nature. Their interactions create the probability for specific opportunities and challenges. Stems can be viewed as energy and Branches as the support for the energy to manifest. Branches provide the foundation and power for Stem qualities to occur. If a detrimental Stem or Branch exists, the negative aspect will manifest. If a beneficial Stem or Branch exists, the positive aspect will manifest. The following section gives more detail about personality characteristics and traits. Once the condition of the Self is determined, evaluate the interactions between Stems and Branches in the Four Pillars and cycles of time.

Stem Combinations

← ——— Day Stems—Elements ———→

Influences ↓	Yang Wood	Yin Wood	Yang Fire	Yin Fire	Yang Earth	Yin Earth	Yang Metal	Yin Metal	Yang Water	Yin Water
A	Yin Water	Yang Water	Yin Metal	Yang Metal	Yin Earth	Yang Earth	Yin Fire	Yang Fire	Yin Wood	Yang Wood
B	Yang Water	Yin Water	Yang Metal	Yin Metal	Yang Earth	Yin Earth	Yang Fire	Yin Fire	Yang Wood	Yin Wood
C	Yin Wood	Yang Wood	Yin Water	Yang Water	Yin Metal	Yang Metal	Yin Earth	Yang Earth	Yin Fire	Yang Fire
D	Yang Wood	Yin Wood	Yang Water	Yin Water	Yang Metal	Yin Metal	Yang Earth	Yin Earth	Yang Fire	Yin Fire
E	Yin Fire	Yang Fire	Yin Wood	Yang Wood	Yin Water	Yang Water	Yin Metal	Yang Metal	Yin Earth	Yang Earth
F	Yang Fire	Yin Fire	Yang Wood	Yin Wood	Yang Water	Yin Water	Yang Metal	Yin Metal	Yang Earth	Yin Earth
G	Yin Earth	Yang Earth	Yin Fire	Yang Fire	Yin Wood	Yang Wood	Yin Water	Yang Water	Yin Metal	Yang Metal
H	Yang Earth	Yin Earth	Yang Fire	Yin Fire	Yang Wood	Yin Wood	Yang Water	Yin Water	Yang Metal	Yin Metal
I	Yin Metal	Yang Metal	Yin Earth	Yang Earth	Yin Fire	Yang Fire	Yin Wood	Yang Wood	Yin Water	Yang Water
J	Yang Metal	Yin Metal	Yang Earth	Yin Earth	Yang Fire	Yin Fire	Yang Wood	Yin Wood	Yang Water	Yin Water

How to use this chart.

1. Find the Day Stem in the Top row of the chart.

2. Move directly below the Day Stem column and find the Hour, Month and Year Stems. Note the letter related to the

intersection of the Day Stem and the Hour, Month and Year Stems.

3. Find the letter and its influence in the following categories.

Stem and Branch Combinations

How to use this chart.

1. Find your Day Stem in the top row of the chart.

2. Look directly below it and find the Branches in the Four Pillars.

3. Write down the number letter and look up the meaning in the following chart.

← ———— Day Element ———— →

Influences ▼	Yang Wood	Yin Wood	Yang Fire	Yin Fire	Yang Earth	Yin Earth	Yang Metal	Yin Metal	Yang Water	Yin Water
A	Rat	Pig	Cock	Monkey	Sheep Ox	Dragon Dog	Horse	Snake	Rabbit	Tiger
B	Pig	Rat	Monkey	Cock	Dragon Dog	Ox Sheep	Snake	Horse	Tiger	Rabbit
C	Rabbit	Tiger	Rat	Pig	Cock	Monkey	Ox Sheep	Dragon Dog	Horse	Snake
D	Tiger	Rabbit	Pig	Rat	Monkey	Cock	Dragon Dog	Dog Sheep	Snake	Horse
E	Horse	Snake	Rabbit	Tiger	Rat	Pig	Cock	Monkey	Ox Dog	Dog Dragon
F	Snake	Horse	Tiger	Rabbit	Pig	Rat	Monkey	Cock	Dragon Dog	Ox Sheep
G	Ox Sheep	Dragon Dog	Horse	Snake	Rabbit	Tiger	Rat	Pig	Cock	Monkey
H	Dragon Dog	Ox Sheep	Snake	Horse	Tiger	Rabbit	Pig	Rat	Monkey	Cock
I	Cock	Monkey	Ox Dog	Dragon Dog	Horse	Snake	Rabbit	Tiger	Rat	Pig
J	Monkey	Cock	Dragon Dog	Ox Sheep	Snake	Horse	Tiger	Rabbit	Pig	Rat

Meaning of the Stem and Branch Combinations

A. Intelligence, academic success and interested in meta-physics. Tendency to be self-interested. Potential to achieve a high level of success in life. Talents in writing and education.

   Positive: Success in the above areas and may obtain fame and high achievements.
   Negative: You may have been spoiled and become dependent on others.

B. High intelligence is used in finding short cuts to success, especially in academics, arts, computers, engineering, architecture and inventions.

   Positive: Very creative and innovative.
   Negative: Can have relationship challenges with your family. Susceptible to cheating or taking short cuts to obtain success.

C. Planners, coordinators, organizers and steady in relationships. If more than one C, there may be divorce. May inherit wealth. Good for marriage prospects.

   Positive: Family provides inheritance, resources and productive background.
   Negative: Tendency toward stubbornness and narrow thinking.

D. Utilizes force or power to manipulate others. Success in time of trouble. Flamboyant, ambitious and very active always needing something to do.

Positive: Success in competitive and physical activities or
   professions.
Negative: Can be abrasive and wild and seek adventure or
   action to satisfy their desires. Problems in relationships.

E. Work hard and earn a steady income. An honest person.

Positive: Can achieve success by being diligent and hard
   working.
Negative: Can be cheap with resources. Difficulties in relationships.

F. You get sudden money but spend it easily. Lots of Romance
and good social life. May marry more than once.

Positive: Potential for wealth and enjoyment of lifestyle.
Negative: Can become lazy, a dreamer and out of touch
   with reality.

G. Enjoy verbal communication but speech may get one in
trouble. Smart and quick witted which can hurt people
when used in a negative way. Many ways to generate
income.

Positive: Strength is assisting or helping people succeed or
   accomplish goals.
Negative: Tendency for too high a drive for success and it
   can turn on them creating self inflicted problems.

H. Enjoy material lifestyle, arts and romance. Enjoy fine arts.
Good chance for steady marriage and family life.

Positive: Enjoyment of life.
Negative: The good life can create health and
   psychological problems.

I. Need to find balance and harmony in life or frustrations will manifest. Ideally you own your own business. Partnerships are difficult, but when you are committed you make it work.

Positive: Success in developing friendships.
Negative: Tendency to get involved in non-productive money making deals and can be emotionally attached to gambling or action.

J. A competitive nature and enjoy being independent and having leadership positions. You do not like being a subordinate or taking orders. You need to control your emotions to be successful in business and romance.

Positive: Best suited for leadership or ownership positions. Can achieve success.
Negative: Can be self-centered and aloof.

Branch to Branch Combinations

The following are the most influential Branch to Branch combinations. These combinations are used in two major ways. The first is when combinations appear in the Four Pillars. In this case the influence lasts for a lifetime. The second is when a cycle of time Branch, for instance, 10 Year Luck Cycle, Annual, Monthly or a Daily Branch combines with the Four Pillars. In this case, the influence lasts for that duration of time.

The following has two sections, the first describes the combinations. The second is a summary table for quick and easy reference.

Good Partners

These Animals are located in the same geographical area and share the same element. They enjoy similar activities and have the potential to become good friends.

1. Snake and Horse. The South and Fire element.
2. Monkey and Cock. The West and Metal Element.
3. Rat and Pig. The North and Water element.
4. Rabbit and Tiger. The East and Wood element.

Trinity

Trinity Branches have a strong affinity and friendship with each other. They are used for romance, marriage and friendships. They release a strong element influence. The Trinity element released can provide beneficial or unfavorable fortune, it will depend on which elements help or hinder the Day Master.

Trinity relationships are Branches which are four locations from each other. There are four sets of three Branches. The following are Trinity relationships.

Branch Combinations	Releases
Cock-Ox-Snake	Metal
Rat-Dragon-Monkey	Water
Rabbit-Sheep-Pig	Wood
Horse-Dog-Tiger	Fire

If 2 are together a mild force is created.

If 3 are together a strong force is created.

Notice the geographical position of the first animal of each Trinity (Diagram 3,). Each is located in the cardinal or middle position. The second and third animals in a Trinity contain the element of the cardinal animal's element, it is in their Hidden elements. When the three Branches of a Trinity combine, it releases the Hidden elements and they become very strong and influential. For example, in the Cock-Snake-Ox combination, Cock is Metal; therefore, the Cock-Ox-Snake Trinity releases Metal. The release of this influence can occur in the Four Pillars, or two may appear in the Four Pillars and one in the 10 Year Luck, Annual or Monthly cycles.

Diagram 3

	South **Red** Snake *Horse* Sheep +Fire -Fire -Earth 6 7 8 **Summer**	
East **Green** Dragon + Earth 5 *Rabbit_* - Wood 4 Tiger + Wood 3 **Spring**		**West** **Gold-Silver** Monkey + Metal 9 *Cock* - Metal 10 Dog + Earth 11 **Fall**
	North **Black-Blue** Ox *Rat* Pig - Earth - Water + Water 2 1 12 **Winter**	

Diagram 4

Trinity relationships are
every fourth Branch or Animal

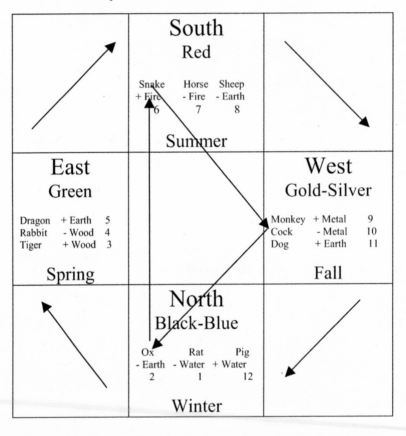

If the change occurs because it is triggered by future cycles of time, for example, two Branches are in the Four Pillars and one is in the Annual Branch, an influence may occur which is very strong, such as a major change from one's normal personality or emotional condition. For most people, sudden change can be very traumatic.

Travelling

Traveling will take place. These are opposite Branch combinations.

1. Snake and Pig. South to North.
2. Tiger and Monkey. East to West.

Playboy or Playgirl

This is often called the four corners or four gates. This combination creates a person who is very sensual, romantic and sexual. They can appear in the Four Pillars which means it represents their constitutional nature, it lasts a lifetime. Also, there can be three in the Pillars and one during a 10 Year Luck, Annual or Monthly cycles, and those qualities last for that time frame.

Each Animal sits in the cardinal or middle geographical location, North, East, South and West.

Horse in South, Cock in West, Rat in North and Rabbit in East.

Opposites Attract

1. Horse and Rat. South to North.
2. Rabbit and Cock. East to West.

These branches are opposite each other and provide a romantic spark, excitement and lots of activity, both positive and negative.

Arguing

These combinations are also named the three Penalties. There will be Arguing, Bickering and Fighting. This occurs in a variety of ways. The first is when the Branches or Animals are side by side in the Birth Pillars. The second is when Pillar Branches interact with 10 Year, Annual or Month cycles.

1. Two Horses
2. Two Cocks
3. Two Pigs
4. Two Dragons

For Example:

	Hour	Day	Month	Year
Stem	Yin Wood	Yin Water	Yang Fire	Yin Fire
Branch	Rabbit	Horse	Horse	Cock

If all four animals combine there will be a serious problem or challenge. It can include any combination of the Four Pillars and cycles of time.

Six Combinations

These Branch combinations pull towards each other and weaken each other's Elemental influence. For example, if the Dragon meets the Rooster, both elements influence is reduced.

1. Rat and Ox combine.
2. Tiger and Pig combine.
3. Rabbit and Dog combine.

4. Dragon and Cock combine.
5. Snake and Monkey combine.
6. Horse and Sheep combine.

Clash

These combinations cause disruptions, challenges and confrontations. The branches are in opposite geographical locations.

1. Rat and Horse.

2. Ox and Sheep.
   These Earths enhance the influence it has on the Four Pillars chart. For example, if it is a beneficial element, it is enhanced.

3. Tiger and Monkey. A lot of Clash activity.

4. Rabbit and Cock.
   Cock (Metal) will usually dominate. If the chart strongly supports Rabbit (Wood), the Rabbit will be the victor.

5. Dragon and Dog. These two Earths facilitate the influence of their element.

6. Snake and Pig. A lot of Clash activity.

Push Out

These combinations are sometimes called the Four Graves, they include only the four Earth Branches, and cause something to be pushed away or kicked out. It can be positive or negative, it depends on which element is stronger. The stronger element will kick the other out. *Good luck* is when the negative element in your chart is kicked out and replaced with a beneficial element.

1. Dragon and Dog
2. Sheep and Ox

Directional Combination

When three elements from the same geographical direction appear a strong elemental influence occurs. The effect of this influence is based on whether the directional element is favorable or unfavorable to the Day Master.

Conflict

These combinations are part of the Four Graves or Earth Branches. They create conflict, turmoil and disruption with each other.

1. Ox and Dog
2. Sheep and Dog

If the Sheep, Dog and Ox combine, there will be a serious obstacle or problem, a person may turn against you.

If the Ox is the Annual Branch and the Sheep is the Month Branch, predict there will be Conflict with your Parents, most likely the Mother.

Branch Combinations

Branch—Animal	Combination	Meaning
Rat	Pig	Good Partner
	Ox	Six Combinations
	Horse	Opposites Attract, Travel, Clash.
	Dog	Romance
	Monkey, Dragon	Trinity
	Horse, Cock, Rabbit	Playboy-Playgirl

Ox	Snake, Cock	Trinity
	Sheep	Push Out, Clash
	Dog	Conflict
	Rat	Six Combinations
	Snake	Push Out

Tiger	Rabbit	Travel, Good Partner
	Monkey	Travel, Clash
	Pig	Six Combinations
	Horse, Dog	Trinity

Rabbit	Tiger	Good Partners
	Sheep, Pig	Trinity
	Dog	Six Combinations
	Cock	Opposites Attract, Clash
	Horse, Cock, Rat	Playboy-Playgirl

Dragon	Dragon	Argue
	Dog	Push Out, Clash
	Rat, Monkey	Trinity
	Cock	Six Combinations

Snake	Horse	Good Partners
	Ox, Cock	Trinity
	Monkey	Six Combinations
	Pig	Travel, Clash

Branch Combinations

Branch—Animal	Combination	Meaning
Horse	Horse	Argue
	Snake	Good Partner
	Dog, Tiger	Trinity
	Sheep	Six Combinations
	Rat	Opposite Attract, Clash
	Cock, Rat, Rabbit	Playboy-Playgirl

Sheep	Ox	Push Out, Clash
	Dog	Conflict
	Rabbit, Pig	Trinity
	Horse	Six Combinations

Monkey	Cock	Good Partners
	Tiger	Travel, Clash
	Dragon, Rat	Trinity
	Snake	Six Combinations

Cock	Cock	Argue
	Monkey	Good Partners
	Rabbit	Opposites Attract, Clash
	Horse, Rat, Rabbit	Playboy-Playgirl
	Snake, Ox	Trinity
	Dragon	Six Combinations

Dog	Dragon	Push Out, Clash
	Ox	Conflict
	Sheep	Conflict
	Horse, Tiger	Trinity
	Rabbit	Six Combinations

Pig	Rat	Good Partners
	Snake	Travel, Clash
	Sheep, Rabbit	Trinity
	Tiger	Six Combinations
	Pig	Argue

Example

Yin Water Day Master
Male born on June 30, 1957 at 6:30 am daylight savings time.

Four Pillars

	Hour	Day	Month	Year
Stem	Yin Wood Offspring 100 X 50%	Yin Water	Yang Fire Grandchild 100 X 100%	Yin Fire Grandchild 100 X 100%
Branch	Rabbit	Cock	Horse	Cock
Elements	Yin Wood Offspring 100 X 50%	Yin Metal Parent 100 X 50%	Yin Fire Grandchild 70 X 100% Yin Earth Grandparent 30 X 50%	Yin Metal Parent 100 X 50%

Branch Combination Analysis

➢Rabbit and Cock: Opposites attract, Clash.

Rabbit, Cock and Horse: are three parts of Playboy-Playgirl type, *Rat* is the fourth. Predict a Rat 10 Year Luck Cycle, Rat Years, or Rat Months, as times for Romance.

➢Cock and Cock: Argue

Stem and Branch Influences

The key to Chinese Astrology is determining the condition of the Day Stem. In general, if the Day Stem receives detrimental energies, the negative aspects of the Stem and Branch combinations manifest. Consequently, that area of life will have stress and obstacles. If the Day Stem receives beneficial energies, the positive aspects will manifest. This principle is applied throughout this Chinese divination system.

Branches are the foundation and set the theme for the cycle of time. Stems are variations within the general theme of a cycle. When a Stem and Branch are in harmony, the effect is very potent.

The following table summarizes the general ways to interpret Stem and Branch influences.

Stem and Branch Type	Meaning
Beneficial Stem and Branch	Primarily good fortune and luck.
Beneficial Stem Detrimental Branch	Primarily unlucky with periods of good fortune.
Detrimental Stem Beneficial Branch	Primarily good fortune with periods of obstacles.
Detrimental Stem and Branch	Primarily unlucky with many challenges.

Chapter 15

Wealth

Wealth is reflected by the element the Day Master or Self controls. For example, a Yang Water Day Stem controls Fire. Fire is the Wealth generator. This represents opportunities to create wealth, prosperity and success. Wealth includes finances, material, education and family. When Wealth generators appear, one must be prepared by having the proper training, energy and resources to turn opportunities into success. Wealth generators can appear in the Four Pillars, 10 Year Luck Cycles, Yearly, Monthly or Daily cycles. The length of an opportunity lasts for the duration of the cycle.

The following are Wealth generators for each element.

Element	Wealth Generator
Water	Fire
Wood	Earth
Fire	Metal
Earth	Water
Metal	Wood

Wealth generators can initiate both positive and negative activities. If one is strong and prepared, Wealth generators create opportunities which may be actualized. If there are too many opportunities, it is possible one may be spread too thin and not maximize opportunities. With this knowledge, one can stay focused and optimize ventures. If one is weak, too many Wealth generators may cause stress, challenges, frustration and fatigue, the reason is it takes energy and resources to act on these Wealth generators. The key is to be prepared when opportunities occur. This is the strength of Chinese Astrology, knowing when opportunities will occur and the condition of the Self. This knowledge will allow you to prepare properly for opportunities.

Wealth generators in the Four Pillars, provide wealth opportunities for a lifetime.

Wealth generators in the 10 Year Luck Cycles, provide opportunities for those 10 years.

Wealth generators in a Year, provide wealth opportunities for that particular year.

Wealth generators for a Month, provide wealth opportunities for that month.

Use time frames with wealth generators to begin or realize wealth activities.

If a Wealth generator is in the Month Branch and the 12 Stage Growth cycle is strong, there is great potential for Wealth; especially from the parents. See the table below.

	Hour	Day	Month	Year
Stem	Sons	Self	Father	Granddad
	Younger Brothers		Older Brothers	Uncles Relatives
Branch	Daughters	Spouse	Mother	Grandmother
	Younger Sisters		Older Sisters	Aunts, Relatives

If the Year Stem has its grandchild in the Four Pillars, a grandparent had wealth or assists you. This is the grandparent's wealth generator.

If the Month Stem has its grandchild in the Four Pillars, a parent had wealth or provides assistance. This is the parent's wealth generator.

If the parent element of the Month Stem or Year Stem is in the pillars, there will be some wealth or support from the family.

If the Self, Month and Year Stems or Branches have the Element they control (Grandchild), there will be wealth in the family.

Chapter 16

Romance

Romance and Marriage are the most asked about topics in astrology. There are a variety of methods to determine how and when Romance and Marriage will manifest in a lifetime. This topic is segmented into two parts. The first portion describes how to predict if Marriage will be beneficial to a person based on their Four Pillars. The second includes a variety of methods to determine compatible partners and the timing of romantic opportunities.

Step 1.

The following Four Pillars chart shows positions of family members. The Day Branch represents the Spouse, and along with the Day Stem is referred to as the Marriage Pillar.

	Hour	Day	Month	Year
Stem	Sons Younger Brothers	Self	Dad Older Brothers	Granddad Uncles Relatives
Branch	Daughters Younger Sisters	Spouse	Mom Older Sisters	Grandmom Aunts Relatives

This analysis centers around the Five Element relationship between the Day Branch, Day Stem and the total Four Pillars chart. The following guidelines assist in predicting how a spouse or marriage will influence life.

1. Compare the Day Branch to the Day Stem.
   This Five Element relationship provides the way in which a couple will interact. In the following example, the Cock is Yin Metal, which is the parent element of the Day Stem, Water. This person's spouse will be nourishing and supporting.

   If the Day Branch was the Dog or Yang Earth, Earth controls Water, the spouse would control, dominate, be more intelligent or older.

	Hour	Day	Month	Year
Stem	Yin Wood Proper Expressions	Yin Water ↑	Yang Fire Primary Wealth	Yin Fire Dynamic wealth
Branch	Rabbit	Cock	Horse	Cock
Elements	Yin Wood Proper Expressions	Yin Metal Inconsistent Resource	Yin Fire Dynamic Wealth Yin Earth Aggressive Power	Yin Metal Inconsistent Resource

2. Compare the Day Branch element to the whole chart.
   Determine the condition of the Self and the beneficial elements. If the Day Branch is a beneficial element, their spouse or marriage will be beneficial to their life. If it is not, a spouse or marriage may cause stress, obstacles and difficulties.

Four Pillars

	Hour	Day	Month	Year
Stem	Yin Wood Offspring 100 X 50%	Yin Water	Yang Fire Grandchild 100 X 100%	Yin Fire Grandchild 100 X 100%
Branch	Rabbit	Cock	Horse	Cock
Elements	Yin Wood Offspring 100 X 50%	Yin Metal Parent 100 X 50%	Yin Fire Grandchild 70 X 100% Yin Earth Grandparent 30 X 50%	Yin Metal Parent 100 X 50%

Total Strenghtening Factor   100

Total Weakening Factor   385

This is a weak Yin Water Day Master and needs to be supported. Beneficial elements are Water and Metal, this person has Metal in the Day Branch, Marriage is beneficial to the whole chart. In totality, a spouse and marriage are good for this person.

Summary

The Five Element relationship between the Day Branch and Day Stem is used to predict how a Spouse and Marriage will influence a person. The first step is evaluating the relationship between the Day Branch and Day Stem. The second step is whether the Day Branch is beneficial to the condition of the Day Stem. The following summarizes the different possibilities.

1. The Day Branch is beneficial to the Day Stem and birth chart. This means a spouse and marriage is good for a person.

2. The Day Branch is beneficial to the Day Stem, but detrimental to the birth chart. A spouse is good for the person, but the marriage is difficult.

3. The Day Branch is detrimental to the Day Stem and birth chart. A spouse and marriage will be difficult.

4. The Day Branch is detrimental to the Day Stem, but beneficial to the birth chart. A spouse creates difficulties, but you enjoy marriage.

Step 2
Methods for determining Romance and Marriage.

1. The most accurate method begins by determining the strength and beneficial elements of the Day Stems of two people. If each person contains their partner's beneficial elements, a deep connection and compatibility exists.

2. *For males*, the element the Self controls, is the Wealth generator. The Wealth generator also represents spouse and romantic opportunities. Time frames with a Wealth generator provide romantic opportunity.

   Example.
   Water Day Stem controls Fire. Fire is the wealth generator and Fire cycles of time provide romantic opportunity.

   For females, the element which controls the Day Stem, represents their spouse and romantic opportunity.

3. The Trinity relationships create an affinity or strong friendship, especially romantic.
   Snake-Cock-Ox.
   Horse, Dog, Tiger.

Sheep, Pig and Rabbit.
Monkey, Rat, Dragon.

4. Branches or Animals in the same geographical areas have an affinity or friendship.
Horse-Snake, South.
Monkey-Cock, West.
Pig-Rat, North.
Tiger-Rabbit, East.

5. Cardinal Positions.
The Rat/North, Rabbit/East, Horse/Fire and Cock/West are in cardinal positions. Each is considered to have "sexual charisma", more than other animals.

6. If a *Horse, Cock, Rat and Rabbit* are in the Four Pillars, this person is a Playboy or Playgirl type. They will flirt and have lots of sexual charisma. Because it is the Four Pillars, it will last throughout a lifetime. If there are three in the Pillars and the other appears in a 10 Year Luck cycle, it will manifest for that time frame.

Chapter 17

Family

To determine how family members influence a person, compare how family pillars affect the Day Stem element. Example 1, is a Four Pillar chart listing family members.

Example 1	Hour	Day	Month	Year
Stem	Sons Younger Brothers	Self	Dad Older Brothers	Granddad Uncles Relatives
Branch	Daughters Younger Sisters	Spouse	Mom Older Sisters	Grandmom Aunts Relatives

Each pillar has Five Elements, compare each pillar element to the Day Stem and evaluate its impact. This will reveal how each family member influences the Self. In example 2, the Parent Pillar has Yang Fire, Yin Fire and Yin Earth, these weaken the Day Stem Water. We can predict the parents created stress, obstacles, difficulties and pressure. The Stems relate to males and the Branches, females. The Month Stem is Yang Fire, with a 100% strength factor, this person's father died when he was an infant. The Month Branch is Yin Fire with a weight of 70 and strength factor of 100%, it also contains a small amount of the controlling element, Yin Earth;

this person's mother died when he was 16. This example is an extreme case, but illustrates this application.

In the Year Pillar, the Grandfather is Yin Fire, providing more Fire, which weakens and creates difficulties. This person never knew his Grandfather, as he passed away before his birth. The Year Branch is Yin Metal, which is the Parent or Resource of the Day Stem. This person had a wonderful relationship with his Grandmother and she was one of the most influential people in his life.

Example 2	Hour	Day	Month	Year
Stem	Yin Wood Offspring 100 X 50%	Yin Water	Yang Fire Grandchild 100 X 100%	Yin Fire Grandchild 100 X 100%
Branch	Rabbit Yin Wood Offspring 100 X 50%	Cock Yin Metal Parent 100 X 50%	Horse Yin Fire Grandchild 70 X 100% Yin Earth Grandparent 30 X 50%	Cock Yin Metal Parent 100 X 50%
Elements				

Another application of Five Element relationships towards family members is to use knowledge of beneficial elements of the Day Stem to determine the influence of the family member. See the examples below for applications.

Example 3

If the Day Stem is weak Water, one needs Metal. If the Month Branch is Metal, which is the Mother of the Day Stem, it provides nourishment. Metal is the "Mother" of Water. The Month Branch is the Mother Pillar, meaning Parents provide nourishment.

Example 3	Hour	Day	Month	Year
Stem		Yin Water		
Branch			Mother Pillar Monkey Yin Metal	

Example 4.

If the Self is weak and the Parents Pillar is the controlling element, Parents will exert a strong pressure, discipline and control. This situation can result in a negative way, because the Self is weak and discipline or control may result in pressure.

Example 5.

If the Self is very strong and the Mother Pillar/Month Branch is the controlling element, the mother provides focus, direction and discipline. In this case the Self is strong enough to use the Control in a positive way.

Example 6.

If the Hour Stem is the mother element of the Self, there is a nourishing relationship between Son and Self.

Example 4	Hour	Day	Month	Year
Stem	Yin Wood	Yang Fire		
Branch				

Applications of the Four Pillars

Hour	Day	Month	Year
Influential people. fellow workers, friends, children, spouse.	Self	Environment, socialization, influences in childhood.	Heritage, genetics, inheritance.

Hour	Day	Month	Year
Inner-Self Internal Dynamics	Inner-self Internal Dynamics	Outer Self External Expression	Outer Self External Expression

Identify the impact of the Five Elements on each area of life. For example, if this person was excess Fire and the Month branch was Horse/Yin Fire, then they would express themselves in a Fiery way. They would be very flamboyant, outgoing, verbal and intense.

If this same person had Yang Water and the Rat/Yin Water in the Hour Pillar, their inner being would be calm and relaxed but they may act like a excess Fire person.

If the Month Pillar was Yang Wood/Tiger, the environment during childhood created pressure and excitement, exacerbating excess Fire condition.

Chapter 18

Five Element Relationships

Upon determining the strength of the Day Master and beneficial elements we can apply universal Five Element relationships to enhance the quality of life. For instance, a weak Water person can design their wardrobe and living environment with beneficial elements, directions, colors and gemstones. The information in the following chart can be applied to one's life based on their Four Pillar astrology. These applications are examples of the integration of the Heaven, Man and Earth.

Element Relationship Chart

Element	Color Primary	Color Secondary	Direction	Organs	Gemstones	Planet
Wood	Green	Blue, Brown	East South East	Liver Gallbladder	Emerald, Jade, Green Opal	Jupiter
Fire	Red	Purple, Pink	South	Heart Small Intestine	Red Ruby	Mars
Earth	Yellow	Beige, Brown	North East South West Center	Spleen Stomach	Yellow Opal, Yellow Diamond	Saturn
Metal	White Gold	Gold Silver Sheen	North West West	Lungs Large Intestine	Pearl, Crystal, White Diamond	Venus
Water	Blue Black	Grey	North	Kidneys Urinary Bladder	White Opal, Blue Sapphire	Mercury

Example

Excess Metal needs Fire. This condition warrants red or pink clothing, living in the Southern Hemisphere, southern part of a country, state or city. One can also spend time in the southern part of their house or wear red ruby gems.

Chapter 19

Four Pillar Example

Male born on June 30, 1957 at 6:30 am daylight savings time.

Four Pillars

	Hour	Day	Month	Year
Stem	Yin Wood Offspring 100 X 50%	Yin Water	Yang Fire Grandchild 100 X 100%	Yin Fire Grandchild 100 X 100%
Branch	Rabbit	Cock	Horse	Cock
Elements	Yin Wood Offspring 100 X 50%	Yin Metal Parent 100 X 50%	Yin Fire Grandchild 70 X 100% Yin Earth Grandparent 30 X 50%	Yin Metal Parent 100 X 50%

10 Year Luck Cycles

Age	0	8	18	28	38	48	58	68	78
Stem	Yang Fire	Yin Wood	Yang Wood	Yin Water	Yang Water	Yin Metal	Yang Metal	Yin Earth	Yang Earth
Branch	Horse	Snake	Dragon	Rabbit	Tiger	Ox	Rat	Pig	Dog
Main Element	Yin Fire	Yang Fire	Yang Earth	Yin Wood	Yang Wood	Yin Earth	Yin Water	Yang Water	Yang Earth
Hidden Elements	Yin Earth	Yang Earth / Yang Metal	Yin Wood / Yin Water		Yang Fire / Yang Earth	Yin Water / Yin Metal		Yang Wood	Yin Metal / Yin Fire

Four Pillar Analysis:

The is a weak Yin Water Day Master. Beneficial elements are Water and Metal. Because there is excess Fire in the Four Pillars, Water is the better element, Water will control Fire and support Water.

Earth, Fire and Wood are detrimental elements, especially in a weak cycle.

Fire represents Wealth and Spouse. When the Day Master is weak, Fire causes stress, pressure and obstacles with Relationships and Money. Because there is substantial Fire, there will be many Wealth and Romantic opportunities. Once again, in a weak cycle, this creates stress and difficulties. The strong Fire in the Month and Year Pillars reflect pressures and difficulties with Parents. The Metal in the Day Branch indicates when the person marries, their spouse will be nourishing. Additionally, Metal is beneficial to the Four Pillars chart, indicating marriage is beneficial to this person. Spouse and Marriage are beneficial.

The predominant Heavenly Influence is Dynamic Wealth. He will generate Wealth in numerous ways. In weak cycles income will be volatile, in strong cycles income will be quick, steady and managed well.

The Hour Pillar is Proper Expression. This represents a strong capacity to create and produce, particularly during a strong cycle.

Branch Combination Analysis

➢ Rabbit and Cock: Opposites attract, Clash.

➢ Rabbit, Cock and Horse are three Branches of the Playboy-Playgirl type, Rat is the fourth. Predict during a Rat 10 Year Luck Cycle, a Rat Year, or a Rat Month, Romance will be in the Air.

➢ Cock and Cock: Argue

Ten Year Luck Cycles

From 0-7 the Month Pillar is utilized. Yang Fire and Horse provide great pressure, stress, weakness and obstacles during childhood and in the environment.

Horse and Cock/Rabbit are 3/4th of Playboy type.

From 8-17 there is a Yin Wood Stem and Snake/Fire Branch, providing weakness, stress and pressure. There is a little Metal in the Hidden elements providing some nourishment. The Snake combines with the two Cocks in the Four Pillars, they are two parts to a trinity and provide some nourishment.

Snake and two Cocks are 2/3rds of Trinity. This releases Metal.

Snake and Horse are good partners.

From 18-27 there is Yang Wood and Dragon. Dragon has Yang Earth, Yin Wood and Yin Water elements. Yang Wood is Powerful Expressions which weakens the Day Master.

Dragon and Cock are one of the six Combinations. They reduce each others influence.

From 28-37 there is Yin Water and Rabbit/Yin Wood. The Yin Water provides nourishment, most of it is in the first five years. The Rabbit is a Clash and opposites attract; this creates excitement, romance, challenges, stimulating activities and romantic break ups.

Rabbit and Cock/Horse are 3/4th of Playboy type.

Rabbit and Cock are Opposites attract and Clash.

From 38-47 the Stem is Yang Water and the Branch is Tiger/Yang Wood. This is a draining and weakening influence. Yang Wood Branch, is the major influence. It is Expressions, if the Day Stem is weak, this energy drains the Day Master. The Yang Water Stems provides support in this cycle.

Tiger and Rabbit are Travel and Good Partner.

Tiger and Horse are 2/3rds of Trinity.

The 48-57 Luck Period changes to provide the energy and elements needed to achieve goals. The Stem Yin Metal, is the mother of Water providing strength. The branch Ox is wet Earth with the Hidden elements Yin Water and Yin Metal. The Cock, Snake and Ox are needed to release the Hidden Yin Metal. The two Cocks in the Birth Pillar along with the 10 Year Luck Cycle Ox, release some of the Yin Metal, providing nourishment and strength.

Ox and Cock are 2/3rds of Trinity.

From 58-77 the auspicious cycle continues. Yang Metal and Rat/Yin Water are beneficial elements and are predominant in these cycles.

Rat and Cock/Horse are 3/4ths of Playboy Type.
Rat and Horse are Opposites attract, Travel and Clash.

The key is whether this person has positioned himself or trained himself to be able to take advantage of this auspicious cycle, beginning at 48. Has he become weak, self-defeated, tired or ready to ride the wave of the most exciting time of life?

Chapter 20

Special Types

Weak Day Masters

In Tzu Ping astrology there are two major types of Birth Charts. The first is a Normal Chart and the second includes a series of Special Charts. Special Charts or "Follow Types" occur when the Day Stem is so weak it cannot retain balance. These "Follow Types" are so weak the Day Master must follow the dominant element in the Four Pillars. Specific conditions must exist for a chart to be classified as a "Follow Type" chart. Power, Expression or Wealth are the three types of special types. They are also called Follow Power, Follow Child and Follow Wealth. The "Follow Element" takes the place of the Day Master as the center piece of the Four Pillars. Apply the principles of Tzu Ping Astrology to the new dominant element. The following are the Special Types.

Special Type Rules
These are general rules for all special types; additional guidelines for each type is located in their separate section.

1. The Day Master has no main root in the Hour, Day, Month or Year Branches. Root is when the Day Stem element is

also found in the Branches. If it is found in the main element of the Branch it is referred to as main root, if it is found in Hidden elements, it is referred as minor root.

2. Minor Root can exist in the Hidden Elements of the Hour, Day and Year Branches, but not the Month Branch.

3. The Day Master Element must not be in Cycle 4 or 5 in the 12 Stage Growth Cycle. Cycle 4 or 5 is referred to as timeliness, which means the element is in a very strong stage and is powerful, too powerful to follow another element in the chart.

4. One of the Five Elements must be dominant in the Chart, it must be located in the Stems, and must be in cycle 4 or 5 in the 12 Stage Growth Cycle. It must be timely.

5. The main element of any of the Four Pillar Branches cannot be the Resource element of the Day Master. A Resource element in the Hidden Elements is allowed. A Resource element in the Stems is allowed, but it can not have root in the branches, either the Main or Hidden Element.

6. The Dominant element cannot have its Power or Grandparent element any where in the Four Pillars.

7. Pay close attention to the Trinity and Directional combinations, they may create a strong element which prevents these Follow Types to manifest.

8. If Earth is the dominant element, the month of birth must be Fire or Earth.

Follow Power

Follow Power has two types, Real Follow Power and Fake Follow Power. The following is Real Follow Power.

Real Follow Power.

- Power or Grandparent element is the dominant element in the Four Pillars.
- Power element must be timely or in stage 4 or 5 in 12 Stage Growth Cycle.
- Expression or Child element can not be in any Stems, or as a main element in any Branch.
- Day Stem element must not be stage 4 or 5 and cannot have main roots. Minor roots may appear anywhere except the Month Branch.
- One Sibling element of the Day Stem may appear in the Stems, but it cannot have any root.
- If the Stems do not have a Sibling element, minor roots may exist in the Hour, Day or Year Branches.
- Beneficial element is Power or Grandparent.
- Expression or Child element is unfavorable unless Wealth or grandchild element is present. This is because the Expression controls Power, when Wealth is present it reduces the energy of Expression because it is Wealth's offspring. Offspring always reduce the parent.
- Wealth generates Power and is beneficial.
- Resource and Sibling are beneficial elements.

Fake Follow Power is similar to Real Follow Power. The difference is the dominant element Power is Stage 1, 6, or 9 in the 12 Stage Growth Cycle. This type is very unbalanced. In good times, great achievement and success can result. In poor luck periods, life is very detrimental. This chart is a great example of a roller-coaster life.

Follow Child
- Expression or child is the dominant element.
- Expression is stage 4 or 5 in 12 Stage Growth Cycle. It is timely.
- The Stems must have one Expression element.
- The Stems cannot have Resource element.
- The main element in the Branches cannot be Resource.
- Sibling with minor root is allowed.
- Wealth element is allowed.
- Day Master can be any location in 12 Stage Growth Cycle.
- Beneficial element is Expression or child.
- Sibling element is beneficial.
- Wealth is beneficial.
- Resource and Power are unfavorable.

Follow Wealth
- Day Master is untimely, not stage 4 or 5 in 12 Stage Growth Cycle.
- Day Master must not have root.
- Wealth element is dominant element and is timely, stage 4 or 5 in 12 Stage Growth Cycle.
- The Stems must have one Wealth element.
- Branches must form a Trinity or Directional Wealth element combination.
- Siblings must not be present in Four Pillars.
- Resource must not be in Stems or as a main element in any Branch.
- Wealth or grandchild element is beneficial element.
- Expression or child element is beneficial element.
- Power or grandchild is neutral.
- Resource and Sibling elements are unfavorable.

Chapter 21

Follow Trend Types

Day Master is too strong.

In these Follow Trend types, the Day Master is too strong and is unable to obtain balance. The way to harmony is to follow the trend or flow of the chart. This means the favorable element will be the Day Master element, not the controlling element, which is normally used to control an excess. This following the Day Stem element or using the Day Stem element as favorable is the key difference. The following lists each of the five Follow Trend Charts.

Wood
• Yin or Yang Wood is the Day Stem.
• Birth Month is Pig, Tiger, Rabbit, Dragon or Sheep.
• Branches must form a Trinity (Pig, Rabbit, Sheep) or Directional combination (Tiger, Rabbit, Dragon).
• Yin or Yang Metal is not in Stems.
• Monkey or Rooster is not in Branches.

Beneficial elements are Wood, Water and Fire.
Unfavorable element is Metal, Earth is unfavorable unless Fire is present.

Fire

- Yin or Yang Fire is the Day Stem.
- Birth Month is Tiger, Snake, Horse, Sheep or Dog.
- Branches form a Trinity (Tiger, Horse, Dog) or Directional combination (Snake, Horse, Sheep).
- Yang or Yin Water is not in the Stems.
- Pig or Rat is not in Branches.

Fire, Wood and Earth are beneficial.

Water and Metal are unfavorable. Metal is favorable if it appears with Earth.

Earth

- Yang or Yin Earth is the Day Stem.
- Earth must be Month Branch.
- The Pillar Branches must be Ox, Dragon, Sheep or Dog.
- Stems cannot have Yang or Yin Wood.

Earth, Fire and Metal are beneficial elements.

Wood is unfavorable. If Water appears with Metal it is favorable, otherwise it is unfavorable.

Metal

- Yang or Yin Metal is Day Stem.
- Birth Month is Snake, Monkey, Cock, Dog or Ox.
- Branches form a Trinity (Snake, Cock, Ox) or Directional Combination (Monkey, Cock, Dog).
- Stems cannot have Yang or Yin Fire.
- Horse or Sheep cannot be in Branches.

Metal, Earth and Water are beneficial.

Fire is unfavorable. Wood is unfavorable unless Water is present.

Water

- Yang or Yin Water is the Day Stem.
- Birth Month is Monkey, Pig, Rat, Ox or Dragon.
- Branches form a Trinity (Monkey, Rat, Dragon) or Directional Combination (Pig, Rat, Ox).
- Stems cannot contain Yang or Yin Earth.
- Branches cannot contain Sheep or Dog.

Wood, Water and Fire are beneficial elements.

Metal is unfavorable. Earth is beneficial when Fire is present, otherwise it is unfavorable.

Conclusion

Chinese Astrology is a mirror, it reflects a way the universe functions. The ancient Chinese perceived the universe as an integrated, living, active and evolving entity. Human life was realized to be a living integration of three major influences: Heaven, Human and Earth. Yin-Yang, Five Elements, Stems, Branches and cycles of time are tools used to evaluate that integration and the influences of nature on human life. Applying the techniques in this book offer a vehicle to deeply understand life. It can be a guide to optimize happiness, health and prosperity. Please enjoy the breadth and depth of this magnificent art.

Appendix

Chinese Astrology Calendar

Made Easy ©

Years 1920-2010

by
David Twicken, Ph.D., L.Ac.

1920

Find yourDay Here	Month		Year				
	Stem	Branch	Stem	Branch	Day	Day	Time
January 6–February 5	Yin Fire	Ox	Yin Earth	Sheep	Jan	54	17:13
February 5–29,–March 6	Yang Earth	Tiger	Yang Metal	Monkey	Feb	25	4:51
March 6–April 5	Yin Earth	Rabbit	Yang Metal	Monkey	Mar	54	10:15
April 5–May 6	Yang Metal	Dragon	Yang Metal	Monkey	April	25	4:12
May 6–June65	Yin Metal	Snake	Yang Metal	Monkey	May	55	9:03
June 6–July 7	Yang Water	Horse	Yang Metal	Monkey	June	26	19:19
July 7–August 8	Yin Water	Sheep	Yang Metal	Monkey	July	56	5:29
August 8–September 8	Yang Wood	Monkey	Yang Metal	Monkey	Aug	27	7:27
September 8–October 8	Yin Wood	Cock	Yang Metal	Monkey	Sep	58	23:33
October 8–November 8	Yang Fire	Dog	Yang Metal	Monkey	Oct	28	1:05
November 8–December 7	Yin Fire	Pig	Yang Metal	Monkey	Nov	59	17:31
December 6–January 6	Yang Earth	Rat	Yang Metal	Monkey	Dec	29	4:34

1921

Find your Day Here	Month		Year				
	Stem	Branch	Stem	Branch	Day	Day	Time
January 6–February 4	Yin Earth	Ox	Yang Metal	Monkey	Jan	60	16:21
February 4–March 6	Yang Metal	Tiger	Yin Metal	Cock	Feb	31	10:46
March 6–April 5	Yin Metal	Rabbit	Yin Metal	Cock	Mar	59	16:09
April 5–May 6	Yang Water	Dragon	Yin Metal	Cock	April	30	10:05
May 6–June 6	Yin Water	Snake	Yin Metal	Cock	May	0	1:05
June 6–July 8	Yang Wood	Horse	Yin Metal	Cock	June	31	14:32
July 8–August 8	Yin Wood	Sheep	Yin Metal	Cock	July	1	18:32
August 8–September 8	Yang Fire	Monkey	Yin Metal	Cock	Aug	32	11:17
September 8–October 9	Yin Fire	Cock	Yin Metal	⚹ Cock	Sep	3	13:10
October 9–November 8	Yang Earth	Dog	Yin Metal	Cock	Oct	33	5:22
November 8–December 8	Yin Earth	Pig	Yin Metal	Cock	Nov	4	7:58
December 8–January 6	Yang Metal	Rat	Yin Metal	Cock	Dec	34	0:17

Branch	Pig	Rat	Ox	Tiger	Rabbit	Dragon	Snake	Horse	Sheep	Monkey	Cock	Dog
Main Element	Yang Water	Yin Water	Yin Earth	Yang Wood	Yin Wood	Yang Earth	Yang Fire	Yin Fire	Yin Earth	Yang Metal	Yin Metal	Yang Earth
Hidden Elements	Yang Wood		Yin Water	Yang Fire		Yin Wood	Yang Earth	Yin Earth	Yin Fire	Yang Earth		Yin Metal
			Yin Metal	Yang Earth		Yin Water	Yang Metal		Yin Wood	Yang Water		Yin Fire

1922

| | Month | | Year | | | | |
Find your Day Here	Stem	Branch	Stem	Branch	Day	Day	Time
January 6–February 4	Yin Metal	Ox	Yin Metal	Cock	Jan	5	10:17
February 4–March 6	Yang Water	Tiger	Yang Water	Dog	Feb	36	22:07
March 6–April 5	Yin Water	Rabbit	Yang Water	Dog	Mar	4	16:34
April 5–May 6	Yang Wood	Dragon	Yang Water	Dog	April	35	21:58
May 6–June 6	Yin Wood	Snake	Yang Water	Dog	May	5	15:53
June 6–July 7	Yang Fire	Horse	Yang Water	Dog	June	36	20:30
July 7–August 8	Yin Fire	Sheep	Yang Water	Dog	July	6	7:13
August 8–September 8	Yang Earth	Monkey	Yang Water	Dog	Aug	37	17:05
September 8–October 9	Yin Earth	Cock	Yang Water	Dog	Sep	8	19:07
October 9–November 9	Yang Metal	Dog	Yang Water	Dog	Oct	38	11:11
November 9–December 7	Yin Metal	Pig	Yang Water	Dog	Nov	9	13:47
December 7–January 6	Yang Water	Rat	Yang Water	Dog	Dec	39	5:11

1923

| | Month | | Year | | | | |
Find your Day Here	Stem	Branch	Stem	Branch	Day	Day	Time
January 6–February 5	Yin Water	Ox	Yang Water	Dog	Jan	10	16:15
February 5–March 6	Yang Wood	Tiger	Yin Water	Pig	Feb	41	4:01
March 6–April 6	Yin Wood	Rabbit	Yin Water	Pig	Mar	9	22:25
April 6–May 6	Yang Fire	Dragon	Yin Water	Pig	April	40	3:46
May 6–June 6	Yin Fire	Snake	Yin Water	Pig	May	10	21:39
June 7–July 8	Yang Earth	Horse	Yin Water	Pig	June	41	2:15
July 8–August 8	Yin Earth	Sheep	Yin Water	Pig	July	11	13:01
August 8–September 9	Yang Metal	Monkey	Yin Water	Pig	Aug	42	22:25
September 9–October 9	Yin Metal	Cock	Yin Water	Pig	Sep	13	1:41
October 9–November 8	Yang Water	Dog	Yin Water	Pig	Oct	43	17:00
November 8–December 8	Yin Water	Pig	Yin Water	Pig	Nov	14	19:30
December 8–January 6	Yang Wood	Rat	Yin Water	Pig	Dec	44	11:05

Branch	Pig	Rat	Ox	Tiger	Rabbit	Dragon	Snake	Horse	Sheep	Monkey	Cock	Dog
Main Element	Yang Water	Yin Water	Yin Earth	Yang Wood	Yin Wood	Yang Earth	Yang Fire	Yin Fire	Yin Earth	Yang Metal	Yin Metal	Yang Earth
Hidden Elements	Yang Wood		Yin Water	Yang Fire		Yin Wood	Yang Earth	Yin Earth	Yin Fire	Yang Earth		Yin Metal
			Yin Metal	Yang Earth		Yin Water	Yang Metal		Yin Wood	Yang Water		Yin Fire

1924

Find your Day Here	Month Stem	Branch	Year Stem	Branch	Day	Day	Time
January 6–February 5	Yin Wood	Ox	Yin Water	Pig	Jan	15	22:06
February 5–March 6	Yang Fire	Tiger	Yang Wood	Rat	Feb	46	9:50
March 6–April 5	Yin Fire	Rabbit	Yang Wood	Rat	Mar	15	4:13
April 5–May 6	Yang Earth	Dragon	Yang Wood	Rat	April	46	9:34
May 6–June 6	Yin Earth	Snake	Yang Wood	Rat	May	16	3:26
June 6–July 7	Yang Metal	Horse	Yang Wood	Rat	June	47	8:02
July 7–August 8	Yin Metal	Sheep	Yang Wood	Rat	July	17	18:32
August 8–September 8	Yang Water	Monkey	Yang Wood	Rat	Aug	48	4:13
September 8–October 8	Yin Water	Cock	Yang Wood	Rat	Sep	19	7:30
October 8–November 8	Yang Wood	Dog	Yang Wood	Rat	Oct	49	21:53
November 8–December 7	Yin Wood	Pig	Yang Wood	Rat	Nov	20	1:26
December 7–January 6	Yang Fire	Rat	Yang Wood	Rat	Dec	50	16:54

1925

Find your Day Here	Month Stem	Branch	Year Stem	Branch	Day	Day	Time
January 6–February 4	Yin Fire	Ox	Yang Wood	Rat	Jan	21	3:54
February 4–March 6	Yang Earth	Tiger	Yin Wood	Ox	Feb	52	15:37
March 6–April 5	Yin Earth	Rabbit	Yin Wood	Ox	Mar	20	10:00
April 5–May 6	Yang Metal	Dragon	Yin Wood	Ox	April	51	15:23
May 6–June 6	Yin Metal	Snake	Yin Wood	Ox	May	21	9:18
June 6–July 8	Yang Water	Horse	Yin Wood	Ox	June	52	13:57
July 8–August 8	Yin Water	Sheep	Yin Wood	Ox	July	22	0:25
August 8–September 7	Yang Wood	Monkey	Yin Wood	Ox	Aug	53	10:08
September 8–October 9	Yin Wood	Cock	Yin Wood	Ox	Sep	24	12:40
October 9–November 8	Yang Fire	Dog	Yin Wood	Ox	Oct	54	3:48
November 8–December 7	Yin Fire	Pig	Yin Wood	Ox	Nov	25	7:16
December 7–January 6	Yang Earth	Rat	Yin Wood	Ox	Dec	55	23:26

Branch	Pig	Rat	Ox	Tiger	Rabbit	Dragon	Snake	Horse	Sheep	Monkey	Cock	Dog
Main Element	Yang Water	Yin Water	Yin Earth	Yang Wood	Yin Wood	Yang Earth	Yang Fire	Yin Fire	Yin Earth	Yang Metal	Yin Metal	Yang Earth
Hidden Elements	Yang Wood		Yin Water	Yang Fire		Yin Wood	Yang Earth	Yin Earth	Yin Fire	Yang Earth		Yin Metal
			Yin Metal	Yang Earth		Yin Water	Yang Metal		Yin Wood	Yang Water		Yin Fire

1926

Find your Day Here	Month Stem	Branch	Year Stem	Branch	Day	Day	Time
January 6–February 4	Yin Earth	Ox	Yin Wood	Ox	Jan	26	9:55
February 4–March 5	Yang Metal	Tiger	Yang Fire	Tiger	Feb	57	21:39
March 5–April 5	Yin Metal	Rabbit	Yang Fire	Tiger	Mar	25	16:00
April 5–May 6	Yang Water	Dragon	Yang Fire	Tiger	April	56	21:19
May 6–June 6	Yin Water	Snake	Yang Fire	Tiger	May	26	15:09
June 6–July 8	Yang Wood	Horse	Yang Fire	Tiger	June	57	19:42
July 8–August 8	Yin Wood	Sheep	Yang Fire	Tiger	July	27	6:06
August 8–September 8	Yang Fire	Monkey	Yang Fire	Tiger	Aug	58	15:45
September 8–October 9	Yin Fire	Cock	Yang Fire	Tiger	Sep	29	18:16
October 9–November 8	Yang Earth	Dog	Yang Fire	Tiger	Oct	59	21:25
November 8–December 8	Yin Earth	Pig	Yang Fire	Tiger	Nov	30	12:08
December 8–January 6	Yang Metal	Rat	Yang Fire	Tiger	Dec	60	4:39

1927

Find your Day Here	Month Stem	Branch	Year Stem	Branch	Day	Day	Time
January 6–February 5	Yin Metal	Ox	Yang Fire	Tiger	Jan	31	15:45
February 5–March 7	Yang Water	Tiger	Yin Fire	Rabbit	Feb	2	3:31
March 7–April 6	Yin Water	Rabbit	Yin Fire	Rabbit	Mar	30	21:51
April 6–May 6	Yang Wood	Dragon	Yin Fire	Rabbit	April	1	3:07
May 6–June 7	Yin Wood	Snake	Yin Fire	Rabbit	May	31	20:54
June 7–July 8	Yang Fire	Horse	Yin Fire	Rabbit	June	2	1:25
July 8–August 8	Yin Fire	Sheep	Yin Fire	Rabbit	July	32	11:50
August 8–September 9	Yang Earth	Monkey	Yin Fire	Rabbit	Aug	3	21:32
September 9–October 9	Yin Earth	Cock	Yin Fire	Rabbit	Sep	34	0:06
October 9–November 8	Yang Metal	Dog	Yin Fire	Rabbit	Oct	4	15:16
November 8–December 8	Yin Metal	Pig	Yin Fire	Rabbit	Nov	35	17:57
December 8–January 6	Yang Water	Rat	Yin Fire	Rabbit	Dec	5	10:27

Branch	Pig	Rat	Ox	Tiger	Rabbit	Dragon	Snake	Horse	Sheep	Monkey	Cock	Dog
Main Element	Yang Water	Yin Water	Yin Earth	Yang Wood	Yin Wood	Yang Earth	Yang Fire	Yin Fire	Yin Earth	Yang Metal	Yin Metal	Yang Earth
Hidden Elements	Yang Wood		Yin Water	Yang Fire		Yin Wood	Yang Earth	Yin Earth	Yin Fire	Yang Earth		Yin Metal
			Yin Metal	Yang Earth		Yin Water	Yang Metal		Yin Wood	Yang Water		Yin Fire

1928

Find your Day Here	Month Stem	Branch	Year Stem	Branch	Day	Day	Time
January 6–February 5	Yin Water	Ox	Yin Fire	Rabbit	Jan	36	21:32
February 5–March 6	Yang Wood	Tiger	Yang Earth	Dragon	Feb	7	9:17
March 6–April 5	Yin Wood	Rabbit	Yang Earth	Dragon	Mar	36	3:38
April 5–May 6	Yang Fire	Dragon	Yang Earth	Dragon	April	7	8:55
May 6–June 6	Yin Fire	Snake	Yang Earth	Dragon	May	37	2:44
June 6–July 7	Yang Earth	Horse	Yang Earth	Dragon	June	8	7:18
July 7–August 8	Yin Earth	Sheep	Yang Earth	Dragon	July	38	17:45
August 8–September 8	Yang Metal	Monkey	Yang Earth	Dragon	Aug	9	3:28
September 8–October 8	Yin Metal	Cock	Yang Earth	Dragon	Sep	40	6:02
October 8–November 8	Yang Water	Dog	Yang Earth	Dragon	Oct	10	21:11
November 8–December 7	Yin Water	Pig	Yang Earth	Dragon	Nov	41	23:50
December 7–January 6	Yang Wood	Rat	Yang Earth	Dragon	Dec	11	4:18

1929

Find your Day Here	Month Stem	Branch	Year Stem	Branch	Day	Day	Time
January 6–February 4	Yin Wood	Ox	Yang Earth	Dragon	Jan	42	3:23
February 4–March 6	Yang Fire	Tiger	Yin Earth	Snake	Feb	13	15:09
March 6–April 5	Yin Fire	Rabbit	Yin Earth	Snake	Mar	41	9:32
April 5–May 6	Yang Earth	Dragon	Yin Earth	Snake	April	12	14:52
May 6–June 6	Yin Earth	Snake	Yin Earth	Snake	May	42	8:41
June 6–July 8	Yang Metal	Horse	Yin Earth	Snake	June	13	13:11
July 8–August 8	Yin Metal	Sheep	Yin Earth	Snake	July	43	23:32
August 8–September 8	Yang Water	Monkey	Yin Earth	Snake	Aug	14	9:09
September 8–October 9	Yin Water	Cock	Yin Earth	Snake	Sep	45	11:40
October 9–November 8	Yang Wood	Dog	Yin Earth	Snake	Oct	15	2:48
November 8–December 7	Yin Wood	Pig	Yin Earth	Snake	Nov	46	5:28
December 7–January 6	Yang Fire	Rat	Yin Earth	Snake	Dec	16	21:57

Branch	Pig	Rat	Ox	Tiger	Rabbit	Dragon	Snake	Horse	Sheep	Monkey	Cock	Dog
Main Element	Yang Water	Yin Water	Yin Earth	Yang Wood	Yin Wood	Yang Earth	Yang Fire	Yin Fire	Yin Earth	Yang Metal	Yin Metal	Yang Earth
Hidden Elements	Yang Wood		Yin Water	Yang Fire		Yin Wood	Yang Earth	Yin Earth	Yin Fire	Yang Earth		Yin Metal
			Yin Metal	Yang Earth		Yin Water	Yang Metal		Yin Wood	Yang Water		Yin Fire

1930

Find Your Day Here	Month Stem	Branch	Year Stem	Branch	Day	Day	Time
January 6–February 4	Yin Fire	Ox	Yin Earth	Snake	Jan	47	9: 03
February 4–March 6	Yang Earth	Tiger	Yang Metal	Horse	Feb	18	20: 52
March 6–April 5	Yin Earth	Rabbit	Yang Metal	Horse	Mar	46	15: 17
April 5–May 6	Yang Metal	Dragon	Yang Metal	Horse	April	17	20: 38
May 6–June 6	Yin Metal	Snake	Yang Metal	Horse	May	47	14: 28
June 6–July 8	Yang Water	Horse	Yang Metal	Horse	June	18	19: 05
July 8–August 8	Yin Water	Sheep	Yang Metal	Horse	July	48	5: 20
August 8–September 8	Yang Wood	Monkey	Yang Metal	Horse	Aug	19	15: 31
September 8–October 9	Yin Wood	Cock	Yang Metal	Horse	Sep	50	17: 29
October 9–November 8	Yang Fire	Dog	Yang Metal	Horse	Oct	20	9: 44
November 8–December 8	Yin Fire	Pig	Yang Metal	Horse	Nov	51	11: 21
December 8–January 6	Yang Earth	Rat	Yang Metal	Horse	Dec	21	9: 32

1931

Find Your Day Here	Month Stem	Branch	Year Stem	Branch	Day	Day	Time
January 6–February 5	Yin Earth	Ox	Yang Metal	Horse	Jan	52	15: 12
February 5–March 7	Yang Metal	Tiger	Yin Metal	Sheep	Feb	23	2: 41
March 7–April 6	Yin Metal	Rabbit	Yin Metal	Sheep	Mar	51	21: 03
April 6–May 7	Yang Water	Dragon	Yin Metal	Sheep	April	22	2: 21
May 7–June 7	Yin Water	Snake	Yin Metal	Sheep	May	52	20: 10
June 7–July 8	Yang Wood	Horse	Yin Metal	Sheep	June	23	: 42
July 8–August 8	Yin Wood	Sheep	Yin Metal	Sheep	July	53	11: 06
August 8–September 9	Yang Fire	Monkey	Yin Metal	Sheep	Aug	24	21: 20
September 9–October 9	Yin Fire	Cock	Yin Metal	Sheep	Sep	55	: 10
October 9–November 8	Yang Earth	Dog	Yin Metal	Sheep	Oct	25	15: 33
November 8–December 8	Yin Earth	Pig	Yin Metal	Sheep	Nov	56	17: 10
December 8–January 6	Yang Metal	Rat	Yin Metal	Sheep	Dec	26	9: 41

Branch	Pig	Rat	Ox	Tiger	Rabbit	Dragon	Snake	Horse	Sheep	Monkey	Cock	Dog
Main Element	Yang Water	Yin Water	Yin Earth	Yang Wood	Yin Wood	Yang Earth	Yang Fire	Yin Fire	Yin Earth	Yang Metal	Yin Metal	Yang Earth
Hidden Elements	Yang Wood		Yin Water	Yang Fire		Yin Wood	Yang Earth	Yin Earth	Yin Fire	Yang Earth		Yin Metal
			Yin Metal	Yang Earth		Yin Water	Yang Metal		Yin Wood	Yang Water		Yin Fire

1932

	Month		Year				
Find Your Day Here	Stem	Branch	Stem	Branch	Day	Day	Time
January 6–February 5	Yin Metal	Ox	Yin Metal	Sheep	Jan	57	3:30
February 5–29,–March 6	Yang Water	Tiger	Yang Water	Monkey	Feb	28	8:30
March 6–April 5	Yin Water	Rabbit	Yang Water	Monkey	Mar	57	2:50
April 5–May 6	Yang Wood	Dragon	Yang Water	Monkey	April	28	8:07
May 6–June 6	Yin Wood	Snake	Yang Water	Monkey	May	58	1:55
June 6–July 7	Yang Fire	Horse	Yang Water	Monkey	June	29	6:28
July 7–August 8	Yin Fire	Sheep	Yang Water	Monkey	July	59	17:14
August 8–September 8	Yang Earth	Monkey	Yang Water	Monkey	Aug	30	3:18
September 8–October 8	Yin Earth	Cock	Yang Water	Monkey	Sep	1	5:03
October 8–November 7	Yang Metal	Dog	Yang Water	Monkey	Oct	31	21:21
November 7–December 7	Yin Metal	Pig	Yang Water	Monkey	Nov	2	: 02
December 7–January 6	Yang Water	Rat	Yang Water	Monkey	Dec	32	15:19

1933

	Month		Year				
Find Your Day Here	Stem	Branch	Stem	Branch	Day	Day	Time
January 6–February 4	Yin Water	Ox	Yang Water	Monkey	Jan	57	2: 24
February 4–March 6	Yang Wood	Tiger	Yin Water	Cock	Feb	28	14: 10
March 6–April 5	Yin Wood	Rabbit	Yin Water	Cock	Mar	57	8: 32
April 5–May 6	Yang Fire	Dragon	Yin Water	Cock	April	28	13: 51
May 6–June 6	Yin Fire	Snake	Yin Water	Cock	May	58	7: 42
June 6–July 7	Yang Earth	Horse	Yin Water	Cock	June	29	12: 18
July 7–August 8	Yin Earth	Sheep	Yin Water	Cock	July	59	23: 02
August 8–September 8	Yang Metal	Monkey	Yin Water	Cock	Aug	30	8: 26
September 8–October 9	Yin Metal	Cock	Yin Water	Cock	Sep	1	11: 47
October 9–November 8	Yang Water	Dog	Yin Water	Cock	Oct	31	3: 11
November 8–December 7	Yin Water	Pig	Yin Water	Cock	Nov	2	5: 51
December 7–January 6	Yang Wood	Rat	Yin Water	Cock	Dec	32	14: 04

Branch	Pig	Rat	Ox	Tiger	Rabbit	Dragon	Snake	Horse	Sheep	Monkey	Cock	Dog
Main Element	Yang Water	Yin Water	Yin Earth	Yang Wood	Yin Wood	Yang Earth	Yang Fire	Yin Fire	Yin Earth	Yang Metal	Yin Metal	Yang Earth
Hidden Elements	Yang Wood		Yin Water	Yang Fire		Yin Wood	Yang Earth	Yin Earth	Yin Fire	Yang Earth		Yin Metal
			Yin Metal	Yang Earth		Yin Water	Yang Metal		Yin Wood	Yang Water		Yin Fire

1934

	Month		Year				
Find Your Day Here	Stem	Branch	Stem	Branch	Day	Day	Time
January 6–February 4	Yin Wood	Ox	Yin Water	Cock	Jan	8	8: 17
February 4–March 6	Yang Fire	Tiger	Yang Wood	Dog	Feb	39	20: 04
March 6–April 5	Yin Fire	Rabbit	Yang Wood	Dog	Mar	7	14: 27
April 5–May 6	Yang Earth	Dragon	Yang Wood	Dog	April	38	22: 44
May 6–June 6	Yin Earth	Snake	Yang Wood	Dog	May	8	13: 31
June 6–July 8	Yang Metal	Horse	Yang Wood	Dog	June	39	18: 02
July 8–August 8	Yin Metal	Sheep	Yang Wood	Dog	July	9	4: 25
August 8–September 8	Yang Water	Monkey	Yang Wood	Dog	Aug	40	14: 04
September 8–October 9	Yin Water	Cock	Yang Wood	Dog	Sep	11	17: 36
October 9–November 8	Yang Wood	Dog	Yang Wood	Dog	Oct	41	7: 45
November 8–December 8	Yin Wood	Pig	Yang Wood	Dog	Nov	12	11: 41
December 8–January 6	Yang Fire	Rat	Yang Wood	Dog	Dec	42	3: 53

1935

	Month		Year				
Find your Day Here	Stem	Branch	Stem	Branch	Day	Day	Time
January 6–February 5	Yin Fire	Ox	Yang Wood	Dog	Jan	13	14: 03
February 5–March 6	Yang Earth	Tiger	Yin Wood	Pig	Feb	44	1: 49
March 6–April 6	Yin Earth	Rabbit	Yin Wood	Pig	Mar	12	20: 11
April 6–May 6	Yang Metal	Dragon	Yin Wood	Pig	April	43	1: 27
May 6–June 7	Yin Metal	Snake	Yin Wood	Pig	May	13	19:12
June 7–July 8	Yang Water	Horse	Yin Wood	Pig	June	44	: 06
July 8–August 8	Yin Water	Sheep	Yin Wood	Pig	July	14	10: 06
August 8–September 8	Yang Wood	Monkey	Yin Wood	Pig	Aug	45	19: 48
September 8–October 9	Yin Wood	Cock	Yin Wood	Pig	Sep	16	23: 25
October 9–November 8	Yang Fire	Dog	Yin Wood	Pig	Oct	46	13: 36
November 8–December 8	Yin Fire	Pig	Yin Wood	Pig	Nov	17	17: 30
December 8–January 6	Yang Earth	Rat	Yin Wood	Pig	Dec	47	9: 43

Branch	Pig	Rat	Ox	Tiger	Rabbit	Dragon	Snake	Horse	Sheep	Monkey	Cock	Dog
Main Element	Yang Water	Yin Water	Yin Earth	Yang Wood	Yin Wood	Yang Earth	Yang Fire	Yin Fire	Yin Earth	Yang Metal	Yin Metal	Yang Earth
Hidden Elements	Yang Wood		Yin Water	Yang Fire		Yin Wood	Yang Earth	Yin Earth	Yin Fire	Yang Earth		Yin Metal
			Yin Metal	Yang Earth		Yin Water	Yang Metal		Yin Wood	Yang Water		Yin Fire

1936

Find your Day Here	Month Stem	Branch	Year Stem	Branch	Day	Day	Time
January 6–February 5	Yin Earth	Ox	Yin Wood	Pig	Jan	18	19:47
February 5–29,–March 6	Yang Metal	Tiger	Yang Fire	Rat	Feb	49	7:30
March 6–April 5	Yin Metal	Rabbit	Yang Fire	Rat	Mar	18	1:50
April 5–May 6	Yang Water	Dragon	Yang Fire	Rat	April	49	7:07
May 6–June 6	Yin Water	Snake	Yang Fire	Rat	May	19	1:14
June 6–July 7	Yang Wood	Horse	Yang Fire	Rat	June	50	5:31
July 7–August 8	Yin Wood	Sheep	Yang Fire	Rat	July	20	15:59
August 8–September 8	Yang Fire	Monkey	Yang Fire	Rat	Aug	51	1:43
September 8–October 8	Yin Fire	Cock	Yang Fire	Rat	Sep	22	5:13
October 8–November 7	Yang Earth	Dog	Yang Fire	Rat	Oct	52	19:33
November 7–December 7	Yin Earth	Pig	Yang Fire	Rat	Nov	23	23:19
December 7–January 6	Yang Metal	Rat	Yang Fire	Rat	Dec	53	15:33

1937

Find your Day Here	Month Stem	Branch	Year Stem	Branch	Day	Day	Time
January 6–February 4	Yin Metal	Ox	Yang Fire	Rat	Jan	24	1:44
February 4–March 6	Yang Water	Tiger	Yin Fire	Ox	Feb	55	13:26
March 6–April 5	Yin Water	Rabbit	Yin Fire	Ox	Mar	23	7:45
April 5–May 6	Yang Wood	Dragon	Yin Fire	Ox	April	54	13:02
May 6–June 6	Yin Wood	Snake	Yin Fire	Ox	May	24	7:02
June 6–July 7	Yang Fire	Horse	Yin Fire	Ox	June	55	11:23
July 7–August 8	Yin Fire	Sheep	Yin Fire	Ox	July	25	21:46
August 8–September 8	Yang Earth	Monkey	Yin Fire	Ox	Aug	56	7:26
September 8–October 9	Yin Earth	Cock	Yin Fire	Ox	Sep	27	11:01
October 9–November 8	Yang Metal	Dog	Yin Fire	Ox	Oct	57	1:12
November 8–December 7	Yin Metal	Pig	Yin Fire	Ox	Nov	28	5:09
December 7–January 6	Yang Water	Rat	Yin Fire	Ox	Dec	58	21:22

Branch	Pig	Rat	Ox	Tiger	Rabbit	Dragon	Snake	Horse	Sheep	Monkey	Cock	Dog
Main Element	Yang Water	Yin Water	Yin Earth	Yang Wood	Yin Wood	Yang Earth	Yang Fire	Yin Fire	Yin Earth	Yang Metal	Yin Metal	Yang Earth
Hidden Elements	Yang Wood		Yin Water Yin Metal	Yang Fire Yang Earth		Yin Wood Yin Water	Yang Earth Yang Metal	Yin Earth	Yin Fire Yin Wood	Yang Earth Yang Water		Yin Metal Yin Fire

1938

| | | Month | | Year | | | | |
Find your Day Here	Stem	Branch	Stem	Branch	Day	Day	Time
January 6–February 4	Yin Water	Ox	Yin Fire	Ox	Jan	29	7: 32
February 4–March 6	Yang Wood	Tiger	Yang Earth	Tiger	Feb	60	19:15
March 6–April 5	Yin Wood	Rabbit	Yang Earth	Tiger	Mar	28	13: 34
April 5–May 6	Yang Fire	Dragon	Yang Earth	Tiger	April	59	18: 49
May 6–June 6	Yin Fire	Snake	Yang Earth	Tiger	May	29	12: 36
June 6–July 8	Yang Earth	Horse	Yang Earth	Tiger	June	60	17: 07
July 8–August 8	Yin Earth	Sheep	Yang Earth	Tiger	July	30	3: 32
August 8–September 8	Yang Metal	Monkey	Yang Earth	Tiger	Aug	1	13: 13
September 8–October 9	Yin Metal	Cock	Yang Earth	Tiger	Sep	32	15: 49
October 9–November 8	Yang Water	Dog	Yang Earth	Tiger	Oct	2	7: 02
November 8–December 8	Yin Water	Pig	Yang Earth	Tiger	Nov	33	9: 49
December 8–January 6	Yang Wood	Rat	Yang Earth	Tiger	Dec	3	3: 13

1939

| | | Month | | Year | | | |
Find your Day Here	Stem	Branch	Stem	Branch	Day	Day	Time
January 6–February 5	Yin Wood	Ox	Yang Earth	Tiger	Jan	34	13: 28
February 5–March 6	Yang Fire	Tiger	Yin Earth	Rabbit	Feb	5	1: 11
March 6–April 6	Yin Fire	Rabbit	Yin Earth	Rabbit	Mar	33	19: 27
April 6–May 6	Yang Earth	Dragon	Yin Earth	Rabbit	April	4	: 38
May 6–June 6	Yin Earth	Snake	Yin Earth	Rabbit	May	34	18: 21
June 6–July 8	Yang Metal	Horse	Yin Earth	Rabbit	June	5	23: 19
July 8–August 8	Yin Metal	Sheep	Yin Earth	Rabbit	July	35	9: 19
August 8–September 8	Yang Water	Monkey	Yin Earth	Rabbit	Aug	6	19: 04
September 8–October 9	Yin Water	Cock	Yin Earth	Rabbit	Sep	37	20: 39
October 9–November 8	Yang Wood	Dog	Yin Earth	Rabbit	Oct	7	14: 05
November 8–December 8	Yin Wood	Pig	Yin Earth	Rabbit	Nov	38	15: 40
December 8–January 6	Yang Fire	Rat	Yin Earth	Rabbit	Dec	8	9: 02

Branch	Pig	Rat	Ox	Tiger	Rabbit	Dragon	Snake	Horse	Sheep	Monkey	Cock	Dog
Main Element	Yang Water	Yin Water	Yin Earth	Yang Wood	Yin Wood	Yang Earth	Yang Fire	Yin Fire	Yin Earth	Yang Metal	Yin Metal	Yang Earth
Hidden Elements	Yang Wood		Yin Water	Yang Fire		Yin Wood	Yang Earth	Yin Earth	Yin Fire	Yang Earth		Yin Metal
			Yin Metal	Yang Earth		Yin Water	Yang Metal		Yin Wood	Yang Water		Yin Fire

1940

Find your Day Here	Month Stem	Branch	Year Stem	Branch	Day	Day	Time
January 6–February 5	Yin Fire	Ox	Yin Earth	Rabbit	Jan	39	19:24
February 5–29,–March 6	Yang Earth	Tiger	Yang Metal	Dragon	Feb	10	7:08
March6–April 5	Yin Earth	Rabbit	Yang Metal	Dragon	Mar	39	1:24
April 5–May 6	Yang Metal	Dragon	Yang Metal	Dragon	April	10	6:35
May 6–June 6	Yin Metal	Snake	Yang Metal	Dragon	May	40	:16
June 6–July 7	Yang Water	Horse	Yang Metal	Dragon	June	11	5:07
July 7–August 8	Yin Water	Sheep	Yang Metal	Dragon	July	41	15:08
August 8–September 8	Yang Wood	Monkey	Yang Metal	Dragon	Aug	12	1:34
September 8–October 8	Yin Wood	Cock	Yang Metal	Dragon	Sep	43	3:30
October 8–November 7	Yang Fire	Dog	Yang Metal	Dragon	Oct	13	19:54
November 7–December 7	Yin Fire	Pig	Yang Metal	Dragon	Nov	44	21:27
December 7–January 6	Yang Earth	Rat	Yang Metal	Dragon	Dec	14	13:58

1941

Find your Day Here	Month Stem	Branch	Year Stem	Branch	Day	Day	Time
January 6–February 4	Yin Earth	Ox	Yang Metal	Dragon	Jan	45	1:04
February 4–March 6	Yang Metal	Tiger	Yin Metal	Snake	Feb	16	12:50
March 6–April 5	Yin Metal	Rabbit	Yin Metal	Snake	Mar	44	7:10
April 5–May 6	Yang Water	Dragon	Yin Metal	Snake	April	15	12:25
May 6–June 6	Yin Water	Snake	Yin Metal	Snake	May	45	6:10
June 6–July 7	Yang Wood	Horse	Yin Metal	Snake	June	16	10:40
July 7–August 8	Yin Wood	Sheep	Yin Metal	Snake	July	46	31:03
August 8–September 8	Yang Fire	Monkey	Yin Metal	Snake	Aug	17	7:22
September 8–October 9	Yin Fire	Cock	Yin Metal	Snake	Sep	48	9:24
October 9–November 8	Yang Earth	Dog	Yin Metal	Snake	Oct	18	1:43
November 8–December 7	Yin Earth	Pig	Yin Metal	Snake	Nov	49	3:25
December 7–January 6	Yang Metal	Rat	Yin Metal	Snake	Dec	19	19:57

Branch	Pig	Rat	Ox	Tiger	Rabbit	Dragon	Snake	Horse	Sheep	Monkey	Cock	Dog
Main Element	Yang Water	Yin Water	Yin Earth	Yang Wood	Yin Wood	Yang Earth	Yang Fire	Yin Fire	Yin Earth	Yang Metal	Yin Metal	Yang Earth
Hidden Elements	Yang Wood		Yin Water	Yang Fire		Yin Wood	Yin Earth	Yin Earth	Yin Fire	Yang Earth		Yin Metal
			Yin Metal	Yang Earth		Yin Water	Yang Metal		Yin Wood	Yang Water		Yin Fire

1942

Find your Day Here	Month Stem	Branch	Year Stem	Branch	Day	Day	Time
January 6–February 4	Yin Metal	Ox	Yin Metal	Snake	Jan	50	7:03
February 4–March 6	Yang Water	Tiger	Yang Water	Horse	Feb	21	18:49
March 6–April 5	Yin Water	Rabbit	Yang Water	Horse	Mar	49	12:53
April 5–May 6	Yang Wood	Dragon	Yang Water	Horse	April	20	18:24
May 6–June 6	Yin Wood	Snake	Yang Water	Horse	May	50	12:07
June 6–July 8	Yang Fire	Horse	Yang Water	Horse	June	21	16:37
July 8–August 8	Yin Fire	Sheep	Yang Water	Horse	July	51	3:14
August 8–September 8	Yang Earth	Monkey	Yang Water	Horse	Aug	22	13:10
September 8–October 9	Yin Earth	Cock	Yang Water	Horse	Sep	53	15:07
October 9–November 8	Yang Metal	Dog	Yang Water	Horse	Oct	23	7:32
November 8–December 8	Yin Metal	Pig	Yang Water	Horse	Nov	54	9:12
December 8–January 6	Yang Water	Rat	Yang Water	Horse	Dec	24	1:47

1943

Find your Day Here	Month Stem	Branch	Year Stem	Branch	Day	Day	Time
January 6–February 5	Yin Water	Ox	Yang Water	Horse	Jan	55	13: 10
February 5–March 6	Yang Wood	Tiger	Yin Water	Sheep	Feb	26	: 41
March 6–April 6	Yin Wood	Rabbit	Yin Water	Sheep	Mar	54	18: 59
April 6–May 6	Yang Fire	Dragon	Yin Water	Sheep	April	25	23: 59
May 6–June 6	Yin Fire	Snake	Yin Water	Sheep	May	55	17: 54
June 6–July 8	Yang Earth	Horse	Yin Water	Sheep	June	26	23: 19
July 8–August 8	Yin Earth	Sheep	Yin Water	Sheep	July	56	9: 03
August 8–September 8	Yang Metal	Monkey	Yin Water	Sheep	Aug	27	18: 19
September 8–October 9	Yin Metal	Cock	Yin Water	Sheep	Sep	58	21: 53
October 9–November 8	Yang Water	Dog	Yin Water	Sheep	Oct	28	13: 21
November 8–December 8	Yin Water	Pig	Yin Water	Sheep	Nov	59	16: 06
December 8–January 6	Yang Wood	Rat	Yin Water	Sheep	Dec	29	7: 33

Branch	Pig	Rat	Ox	Tiger	Rabbit	Dragon	Snake	Horse	Sheep	Monkey	Cock	Dog
Main Element	Yang Water	Yin Water	Yin Earth	Yang Wood	Yin Wood	Yang Earth	Yang Fire	Yin Fire	Yin Earth	Yang Metal	Yin Metal	Yang Earth
Hidden Elements	Yang Wood		Yin Water	Yang Fire		Yin Wood	Yang Earth	Yin Earth	Yin Fire	Yang Earth		Yin Metal
			Yin Metal	Yang Earth		Yin Water	Yang Metal		Yin Wood	Yang Water		Yin Fire

1944

	Month		Year				
Find your Day Here	Stem	Branch	Stem	Branch	Day	Day	Time
January 6–February 5	Yin Wood	Ox	Yin Water	Sheep	Jan	60	19:00
February 5–29,–March 6	Yang Fire	Tiger	Yang Wood	Monkey	Feb	31	6:23
March 6–April 5	Yin Fire	Rabbit	Yang Wood	Monkey	Mar	60	:41
April 5–May 6	Yang Earth	Dragon	Yang Wood	Monkey	April	31	5:54
May 6–June 6	Yin Earth	Snake	Yang Wood	Monkey	May	1	23:40
June 6–July 7	Yang Metal	Horse	Yang Wood	Monkey	June	32	4:11
July 7–August 8	Yin Metal	Sheep	Yang Wood	Monkey	July	2	14:37
August 8–September 8	Yang Water	Monkey	Yang Wood	Monkey	Aug	33	:19
September 8–October 8	Yin Water	Cock	Yang Wood	Monkey	Sep	4	3:42
October 8–November 7	Yang Wood	Dog	Yang Wood	Monkey	Oct	34	19:10
November 7–December 7	Yin Wood	Pig	Yang Wood	Monkey	Nov	5	21:55
December 7–January 6	Yang Fire	Rat	Yang Wood	Monkey	Dec	35	13:28

1945

	Month		Year				
Find your Day Here	Stem	Branch	Stem	Branch	Day	Day	Time
January 6–February 4	Yin Fire	Ox	Yang Wood	Monkey	Jan	6	:35
February 4–March 6	Yang Earth	Tiger	Yin Wood	Cock	Feb	37	21:20
March 6–April 5	Yin Earth	Rabbit	Yin Wood	Cock	Mar	5	6:38
April 5–May 6	Yang Metal	Dragon	Yin Wood	Cock	April	36	11:52
May 6–June 6	Yin Metal	Snake	Yin Wood	Cock	May	6	5:37
June 6–July 7	Yang Water	Horse	Yin Wood	Cock	June	37	10:06
July 7–August 8	Yin Water	Sheep	Yin Wood	Cock	July	7	20:27
August 8–September 8	Yang Wood	Monkey	Yin Wood	Cock	Aug	38	6:06
September 8–October 9	Yin Wood	Cock	Yin Wood	Cock	Sep	9	9:30
October 9–November 8	Yang Fire	Dog	Yin Wood	Cock	Oct	39	:59
November 8–December 7	Yin Fire	Pig	Yin Wood	Cock	Nov	10	3:44
December 7–January 6	Yang Earth	Rat	Yin Wood	Cock	Dec	40	19:18

Branch	Pig	Rat	Ox	Tiger	Rabbit	Dragon	Snake	Horse	Sheep	Monkey	Cock	Dog
Main Element	Yang Water	Yin Water	Yin Earth	Yang Wood	Yin Wood	Yang Earth	Yang Fire	Yin Fire	Yin Earth	Yang Metal	Yin Metal	Yang Earth
Hidden Elements	Yang Wood		Yin Water	Yang Fire		Yin Wood	Yang Earth	Yin Earth	Yin Fire	Yang Earth		Yin Metal
			Yin Metal	Yang Earth		Yin Water	Yang Metal		Yin Wood	Yang Water		Yin Fire

1946

Find your Day Here	Month Stem	Branch	Year Stem	Branch	Day	Day	Time
January 6–February 4	Yin Earth	Ox	Yin Wood	Cock	Jan	11	6:17
February 4–March 6	Yang Metal	Tiger	Yang Fire	Dog	Feb	42	18:05
March 6–April 5	Yin Metal	Rabbit	Yang Fire	Dog	Mar	10	12:25
April 5–May 6	Yang Water	Dragon	Yang Fire	Dog	April	41	17:39
May 6–June 6	Yin Water	Snake	Yang Fire	Dog	May	11	11:22
June 6–July 8	Yang Wood	Horse	Yang Fire	Dog	June	42	15:49
July 8–August 8	Yin Wood	Sheep	Yang Fire	Dog	July	12	2:11
August 8–September 8	Yang Fire	Monkey	Yang Fire	Dog	Aug	43	11:52
September 8–October 9	Yin Fire	Cock	Yang Fire	Dog	Sep	14	15:18
October 9–November 8	Yang Earth	Dog	Yang Fire	Dog	Oct	44	5:42
November 8–December 8	Yin Earth	Pig	Yang Fire	Dog	Nov	15	9:34
December 8–January 6	Yang Metal	Rat	Yang Fire	Dog	Dec	45	1:01

1947

Find your Day Here	Month Stem	Branch	Year Stem	Branch	Day	Day	Time
January 6–February 5	Yin Metal	Ox	Yang Fire	Dog	Jan	16	12:11
February 5–March 6	Yang Water	Tiger	Yin Fire	Pig	Feb	47	23:55
March 6–April 6	Yin Water	Rabbit	Yin Fire	Pig	Mar	15	18:12
April 6–May 6	Yang Wood	Dragon	Yin Fire	Pig	April	46	23:23
May 6–June 6	Yin Wood	Snake	Yin Fire	Pig	May	16	17:05
June 6–July 8	Yang Fire	Horse	Yin Fire	Pig	June	47	21:33
July 8–August 8	Yin Fire	Sheep	Yin Fire	Pig	July	17	7:56
August 8–September 8	Yang Earth	Monkey	Yin Fire	Pig	Aug	48	17:39
September 8–October 9	Yin Earth	Cock	Yin Fire	Pig	Sep	19	21:07
October 9–November 8	Yang Metal	Dog	Yin Fire	Pig	Oct	49	11:32
November 8–December 8	Yin Metal	Pig	Yin Fire	Pig	Nov	20	15:23
December 8–January 6	Yang Water	Rat	Yin Fire	Pig	Dec	50	7:40

Branch	Pig	Rat	Ox	Tiger	Rabbit	Dragon	Snake	Horse	Sheep	Monkey	Cock	Dog
Main Element	Yang Water	Yin Water	Yin Earth	Yang Wood	Yin Wood	Yang Earth	Yang Fire	Yin Fire	Yin Earth	Yang Metal	Yin Metal	Yang Earth
Hidden Elements	Yang Wood		Yin Water	Yang Fire		Yin Wood	Yang Earth	Yin Earth	Yin Fire	Yang Earth		Yin Metal
			Yin Metal	Yang Earth		Yin Water	Yang Metal		Yin Wood	Yang Water		Yin Fire

1948

Find your Day Here	Month Stem	Branch	Year Stem	Branch	Day	Day	Time
January 6–February 5	Yin Water	Ox	Yin Fire	Pig	Jan	21	18:01
February 5–29,–March 6	Yang Wood	Tiger	Yang Earth	Rat	Feb	52	5:43
March 6–April 5	Yin Wood	Rabbit	Yang Earth	Rat	Mar	21	23:58
April 5–May 5	Yang Fire	Dragon	Yang Earth	Rat	April	52	5:10
May 5–June 6	Yin Fire	Snake	Yang Earth	Rat	May	22	22:53
June 6–July 7	Yang Earth	Horse	Yang Earth	Rat	June	53	3:21
July 7–August 8	Yin Earth	Sheep	Yang Earth	Rat	July	23	13:44
August 8–September 8	Yang Metal	Monkey	Yang Earth	Rat	Aug	54	23:27
September 8–October 8	Yin Metal	Cock	Yang Earth	Rat	Sep	25	2:06
October 8–November 7	Yang Water	Dog	Yang Earth	Rat	Oct	55	17:21
November 7–December 7	Yin Water	Pig	Yang Earth	Rat	Nov	26	21:12
December 7–January 6	Yang Wood	Rat	Yang Earth	Rat	Dec	56	13:29

1949

Find your Day Here	Month Stem	Branch	Year Stem	Branch	Day	Day	Time
January 6–February 4	Yin Wood	Ox	Yang Earth	Rat	Jan	27	:08
February 4–March 6	Yang Fire	Tiger	Yin Earth	Ox	Feb	58	11:23
March 6–April 5	Yin Fire	Rabbit	Yin Earth	Ox	Mar	26	5:40
April 5–May 6	Yang Earth	Dragon	Yin Earth	Ox	April	57	10:52
May 6–June 6	Yin Earth	Snake	Yin Earth	Ox	May	27	4:37
June 6–July 7	Yang Metal	Horse	Yin Earth	Ox	June	58	9:07
July 7–August 8	Yin Metal	Sheep	Yin Earth	Ox	July	28	19:32
August 8–September 8	Yang Water	Monkey	Yin Earth	Ox	Aug	59	5:16
September 8–October 8	Yin Water	Cock	Yin Earth	Ox	Sep	30	7:55
October 8–November 8	Yang Wood	Dog	Yin Earth	Ox	Oct	60	:15
November 8–December 7	Yin Wood	Pig	Yin Earth	Ox	Nov	31	3:02
December 7–January 6	Yang Fire	Rat	Yin Earth	Ox	Dec	1	19:20

Branch	Pig	Rat	Ox	Tiger	Rabbit	Dragon	Snake	Horse	Sheep	Monkey	Cock	Dog
Main Element	Yang Water	Yin Water	Yin Earth	Yang Wood	Yin Wood	Yang Earth	Yang Fire	Yin Fire	Yin Earth	Yang Metal	Yin Metal	Yang Earth
Hidden Elements	Yang Wood		Yin Water	Yang Fire		Yin Wood	Yang Earth	Yin Earth	Yin Fire	Yang Earth		Yin Metal
			Yin Metal	Yang Earth		Yin Water	Yang Metal		Yin Wood	Yang Water		Yin Fire

1950

Find your Day Here	Month Stem	Branch	Year Stem	Branch	Day	Day	Time
January 6–February 4	Yin Fire	Ox	Yin Earth	Ox	Jan	32	5: 39
February 4–March 6	Yang Earth	Tiger	Yang Metal	Tiger	Feb	3	17: 21
March 6–April 5	Yin Earth	Rabbit	Yang Metal	Tiger	Mar	31	11: 36
April 5–May 6	Yang Metal	Dragon	Yang Metal	Tiger	April	2	16: 45
May 6–June 6	Yin Metal	Snake	Yang Metal	Tiger	May	32	10: 25
June 6–July 8	Yang Water	Horse	Yang Metal	Tiger	June	3	15: 09
July 8–August 8	Yin Water	Sheep	Yang Metal	Tiger	July	33	1: 14
August 8–September 8	Yang Wood	Monkey	Yang Metal	Tiger	Aug	4	11: 36
September 8–October 9	Yin Wood	Cock	Yang Metal	Tiger	Sep	35	13: 34
October 9–November 8	Yang Fire	Dog	Yang Metal	Tiger	Oct	5	6: 04
November 8–December 8	Yin Fire	Pig	Yang Metal	Tiger	Nov	36	7: 44
December 8–January 6	Yang Earth	Rat	Yang Metal	Tiger	Dec	6	1: 10

1951

Find your Day Here	Month Stem	Branch	Year Stem	Branch	Day	Day	Time
January 6–February 4	Yin Earth	Ox	Yang Metal	Tiger	Jan	37	11:31
February 4–March 6	Yang Metal	Tiger	Yin Metal	Rabbit	Feb	8	23:14
March 6–April 5	Yin Metal	Rabbit	Yin Metal	Rabbit	Mar	36	17:27
April 5–May 6	Yang Water	Dragon	Yin Metal	Rabbit	April	7	22:33
May 6–June 6	Yin Water	Snake	Yin Metal	Rabbit	May	37	16:10
June 6–July 8	Yang Wood	Horse	Yin Metal	Rabbit	June	8	20:33
July 8–August 8	Yin Wood	Sheep	Yin Metal	Rabbit	July	38	7:28
August 8–September 8	Yang Fire	Monkey	Yin Metal	Rabbit	Aug	9	17:24
September 8–October 9	Yin Fire	Cock	Yin Metal	Rabbit	Sep	40	19:19
October 9–November 8	Yang Earth	Dog	Yin Metal	Rabbit	Oct	10	11:53
November 8–December 8	Yin Earth	Pig	Yin Metal	Rabbit	Nov	41	13:27
December 8–January 6	Yang Metal	Rat	Yin Metal	Rabbit	Dec	11	6:03

Branch	Pig	Rat	Ox	Tiger	Rabbit	Dragon	Snake	Horse	Sheep	Monkey	Cock	Dog
Main Element	Yang Water	Yin Water	Yin Earth	Yang Wood	Yin Wood	Yang Earth	Yang Fire	Yin Fire	Yin Earth	Yang Metal	Yin Metal	Yang Earth
Hidden Elements	Yang Wood		Yin Water	Yang Fire		Yin Wood	Yang Earth	Yin Earth	Yin Fire	Yang Earth		Yin Metal
			Yin Metal	Yang Earth		Yin Water	Yang Metal		Yin Wood	Yang Water		Yin Fire

1952

Find your Day Here	Month Stem	Branch	Year Stem	Branch	Day	Day	Time
January 6–February 5	Yin Metal	Ox	Yin Metal	Rabbit	Jan	42	17:10
February 5–29,–March 6	Yang Water	Tiger	Yang Water	Dragon	Feb	13	4:54
March 6–April 5	Yin Water	Rabbit	Yang Water	Dragon	Mar	42	23:08
April 5–May 5	Yang Wood	Dragon	Yang Water	Dragon	April	13	4:16
May 5–June 6	Yin Wood	Snake	Yang Water	Dragon	May	43	21:54
June 6–July 7	Yang Fire	Horse	Yang Water	Dragon	June	14	2:21
July 7–August 7	Yin Fire	Sheep	Yang Water	Dragon	July	44	13:15
August 7–September 8	Yang Earth	Monkey	Yang Water	Dragon	Aug	15	23:12
September 8–October 8	Yin Earth	Cock	Yang Water	Dragon	Sep	46	1:14
October 8–November 7	Yang Metal	Dog	Yang Water	Dragon	Oct	16	17:42
November 7–December 7	Yin Metal	Pig	Yang Water	Dragon	Nov	47	19:22
December 7–January 6	Yang Water	Rat	Yang Water	Dragon	Dec	17	11:56

1953

Find your Day Here	Month Stem	Branch	Year Stem	Branch	Day	Day	Time
January 5–February 4	Yin Water	Ox	Yang Water	Dragon	Jan	48	23: 03
February 4–March 6	Yang Wood	Tiger	Yin Water	Snake	Feb	19	10: 46
March 6–April 5	Yin Wood	Rabbit	Yin Water	Snake	Mar	47	4: 56
April 5–May 6	Yang Fire	Dragon	Yin Water	Snake	April	18	10: 13
May 6–June 6	Yin Fire	Snake	Yin Water	Snake	May	48	3: 53
June 6–July 8	Yang Earth	Horse	Yin Water	Snake	June	19	8: 17
July 8–August 8	Yin Earth	Sheep	Yin Water	Snake	July	49	19: 03
August 8–September 8	Yang Metal	Monkey	Yin Water	Snake	Aug	20	5: 00
September 8–October 8	Yin Metal	Cock	Yin Water	Snake	Sep	51	7: 59
October 8–November 8	Yang Water	Dog	Yin Water	Snake	Oct	21	23: 31
November 8–December 7	Yin Water	Pig	Yin Water	Snake	Nov	52	1: 02
December 7–January 6	Yang Wood	Rat	Yin Water	Snake	Dec	22	17: 38

Branch	Pig	Rat	Ox	Tiger	Rabbit	Dragon	Snake	Horse	Sheep	Monkey	Cock	Dog
Main Element	Yang Water	Yin Water	Yin Earth	Yang Wood	Yin Wood	Yang Earth	Yang Fire	Yin Fire	Yin Earth	Yang Metal	Yin Metal	Yang Earth
Hidden Elements	Yang Wood		Yin Water	Yang Fire		Yin Wood	Yang Earth	Yin Earth	Yin Fire	Yang Earth		Yin Metal
			Yin Metal	Yang Earth		Yin Water	Yang Metal		Yin Wood	Yang Water		Yin Fire

1954

Find your Day Here	Month Stem	Branch	Year Stem	Branch	Day	Day	Time
January 6–February 4	Yin Wood	Ox	Yin Water	Snake	Jan	53	5:18
February 4–March 6	Yang Fire	Tiger	Yang Wood	Horse	Feb	24	16:31
March 6–April 5	Yin Fire	Rabbit	Yang Wood	Horse	Mar	52	10:29
April 5–May 6	Yang Earth	Dragon	Yang Wood	Horse	April	23	16:00
May 6–June 6	Yin Earth	Snake	Yang Wood	Horse	May	53	9:39
June 6–July 8	Yang Metal	Horse	Yang Wood	Horse	June	24	14:02
July 8–August 8	Yin Metal	Sheep	Yang Wood	Horse	July	54	:20
August 8–September 8	Yang Water	Monkey	Yang Wood	Horse	Aug	25	10:00
September 8–October 9	Yin Water	Cock	Yang Wood	Horse	Sep	56	13:47
October 9–November 8	Yang Wood	Dog	Yang Wood	Horse	Oct	26	5:20
November 8–December 8	Yin Wood	Pig	Yang Wood	Horse	Nov	57	8:09
December 8–January 6	Yang Fire	Rat	Yang Wood	Horse	Dec	27	:28

1955

Find your Day Here	Month Stem	Branch	Year Stem	Branch	Day	Day	Time
January 6–February 4	Yin Fire	Ox	Yang Wood	Horse	Jan	58	11:08
February 4–March 6	Yang Earth	Tiger	Yin Wood	Sheep	Feb	29	22:18
March 6–April 5	Yin Earth	Rabbit	Yin Wood	Sheep	Mar	57	16:32
April 5–May 6	Yang Metal	Dragon	Yin Wood	Sheep	April	28	21:39
May 6–June 6	Yin Metal	Snake	Yin Wood	Sheep	May	58	15:18
June 6–July 8	Yang Water	Horse	Yin Wood	Sheep	June	29	19:44
July 8–August 8	Yin Water	Sheep	Yin Wood	Sheep	July	59	6:07
August 8–September 8	Yang Wood	Monkey	Yin Wood	Sheep	Aug	30	15:50
September 8–October 9	Yin Wood	Cock	Yin Wood	Sheep	Sep	1	19:36
October 9–November 8	Yang Fire	Dog	Yin Wood	Sheep	Oct	31	11:09
November 8–December 8	Yin Fire	Pig	Yin Wood	Sheep	Nov	2	13:49
December 8–January 6	Yang Earth	Rat	Yin Wood	Sheep	Dec	32	5:23

Branch	Pig	Rat	Ox	Tiger	Rabbit	Dragon	Snake	Horse	Sheep	Monkey	Cock	Dog
Main Element	Yang Water	Yin Water	Yin Earth	Yang Wood	Yin Wood	Yang Earth	Yang Fire	Yin Fire	Yin Earth	Yang Metal	Yin Metal	Yang Earth
Hidden Elements	Yang Wood		Yin Water	Yang Fire		Yin Wood	Yang Earth	Yin Earth	Yin Fire	Yang Earth		Yin Metal
			Yin Metal	Yang Earth		Yin Water	Yang Metal		Yin Wood	Yang Water		Yin Fire

1956

	Month		Year				
Find your Day Here	Stem	Branch	Stem	Branch	Day	Day	Time
January 6–February 5	Yin Earth	Ox	Yin Wood	Sheep	Jan	3	16:31
February 5–29, March 5	Yang Metal	Tiger	Yang Fire	Monkey	Feb	34	4:13
March 5–April 5	Yin Metal	Rabbit	Yang Fire	Monkey	Mar	3	22:25
April 5–May 5	Yang Water	Dragon	Yang Fire	Monkey	April	34	3:32
May 5–June 6	Yin Water	Snake	Yang Fire	Monkey	May	4	21:11
June 6–July 7	Yang Wood	Horse	Yang Fire	Monkey	June	35	1:36
July 7–August 7	Yin Wood	Sheep	Yang Fire	Monkey	July	5	11:59
August 7–September 8	Yang Fire	Monkey	Yang Fire	Monkey	Aug	36	21:41
September 8–October 8	Yin Fire	Cock	Yang Fire	Monkey	Sep	7	1:24
October 8–November 7	Yang Earth	Dog	Yang Fire	Monkey	Oct	37	15:37
November 7–December 7	Yin Earth	Pig	Yang Fire	Monkey	Nov	8	19:48
December 7–January 5	Yang Metal	Rat	Yang Fire	Monkey	Dec	38	11:03

1957

	Month		Year				
Find your Day Here	Stem	Branch	Stem	Branch	Day	Day	Time
January 5–February 4	Yin Metal	Ox	Yang Fire	Monkey	Jan	4	22:11
February 4–March 6	Yang Water	Tiger	Yin Fire	Cock	Feb	40	9:55
March 6–April 5	Yin Water	Rabbit	Yin Fire	Cock	Mar	8	4:11
April 5–May 6	Yang Wood	Dragon	Yin Fire	Cock	April	39	9:19
May 6–June 6	Yin Wood	Snake	Yin Fire	Cock	May	9	3:11
June 6–July 7	Yang Fire	Horse	Yin Fire	Cock	June	40	7:25
July 7–August 8	Yin Fire	Sheep	Yin Fire	Cock	July	10	17:49
August 8–September 8	Yang Earth	Monkey	Yin Fire	Cock	Aug	41	3:33
September 8–October 8	Yin Earth	Cock	Yin Fire	Cock	Sep	12	7:03
October 8–November 8	Yang Metal	Dog	Yin Fire	Cock	Oct	42	21:31
November 8–December 7	Yin Metal	Pig	Yin Fire	Cock	Nov	13	1:37
December 7–January 6	Yang Water	Rat	Yin Fire	Cock	Dec	43	17:57

Branch	Pig	Rat	Ox	Tiger	Rabbit	Dragon	Snake	Horse	Sheep	Monkey	Cock	Dog
Main Element	Yang Water	Yin Water	Yin Earth	Yang Wood	Yin Wood	Yang Earth	Yang Fire	Yin Fire	Yin Earth	Yang Metal	Yin Metal	Yang Earth
Hidden Elements	Yang Wood		Yin Water	Yang Fire		Yin Wood	Yang Earth	Yin Earth	Yin Fire	Yang Earth		Yin Metal
			Yin Metal	Yang Earth		Yin Water	Yang Metal		Yin Wood	Yang Water		Yin Fire

1958

Find your Day Here	Month Stem	Branch	Year Stem	Branch	Day	Day	Time
January 6–February 4	Yin Water	Ox	Yin Fire	Cock	Jan	14	4: 05
February 4–March 6	Yang Wood	Tiger	Yang Earth	Dog	Feb	45	15: 50
March 6–April 5	Yin Wood	Rabbit	Yang Earth	Dog	Mar	13	10: 06
April 5–May 6	Yang Fire	Dragon	Yang Earth	Dog	April	44	15: 13
May 6–June 6	Yin Fire	Snake	Yang Earth	Dog	May	14	9: 01
June 6–July 8	Yang Earth	Horse	Yang Earth	Dog	June	45	13: 13
July 8–August 8	Yin Earth	Sheep	Yang Earth	Dog	July	15	: 03
August 8–September 8	Yang Metal	Monkey	Yang Earth	Dog	Aug	46	9: 18
September 8–October 9	Yin Metal	Cock	Yang Earth	Dog	Sep	17	13: 01
October 9–November 8	Yang Water	Dog	Yang Earth	Dog	Oct	47	3: 20
November 8–December 7	Yin Water	Pig	Yang Earth	Dog	Nov	18	7: 26
December 7–January 6	Yang Wood	Rat	Yang Earth	Dog	Dec	48	23: 47

1959

Find your Day Here	Month Stem	Branch	Year Stem	Branch	Day	Day	Time
January 6–February 4	Yin Wood	Ox	Yang Earth	Dog	Jan	19	9: 59
February 4–March 6	Yang Fire	Tiger	Yin Earth	Pig	Feb	50	21: 43
March 6–April 5	Yin Fire	Rabbit	Yin Earth	Pig	Mar	18	15: 57
April 5–May 6	Yang Earth	Dragon	Yin Earth	Pig	April	49	21: 04
May 6–June 6	Yin Earth	Snake	Yin Earth	Pig	May	19	14: 39
June 6–July 8	Yang Metal	Horse	Yin Earth	Pig	June	50	19: 01
July 8–August 8	Yin Metal	Sheep	Yin Earth	Pig	July	20	5: 21
August 8–September 8	Yang Water	Monkey	Yin Earth	Pig	Aug	51	15: 05
September 8–October 8	Yin Water	Cock	Yin Earth	Pig	Sep	22	17: 49
October 9–November 8	Yang Wood	Dog	Yin Earth	Pig	Oct	52	9: 11
November 8–December 8	Yin Wood	Pig	Yin Earth	Pig	Nov	23	13: 16
December 8–January 6	Yang Fire	Rat	Yin Earth	Pig	Dec	53	5: 37

Branch	Pig	Rat	Ox	Tiger	Rabbit	Dragon	Snake	Horse	Sheep	Monkey	Cock	Dog
Main Element	Yang Water	Yin Water	Yin Earth	Yang Wood	Yin Wood	Yang Earth	Yang Fire	Yang Fire	Yin Earth	Yang Metal	Yin Metal	Yang Earth
Hidden Elements	Yang Wood		Yin Water	Yang Fire		Yin Wood	Yang Earth	Yin Earth	Yin Fire	Yang Earth		Yin Metal
			Yin Metal	Yang Earth		Yin Water	Yang Metal		Yin Wood	Yang Water		Yin Fire

1960

Find your Day Here	Month Stem	Branch	Year Stem	Branch	Day	Day	Time
January 6 – February 5	Yin Fire	Ox	Yin Earth	Pig	Jan	24	15: 43
February 5 –29, March 5	Yang Earth	Tiger	Yang Metal	Rat	Feb	55	3: 23
March 5 - April 5	Yin Earth	Rabbit	Yang Metal	Rat	Mar	24	21: 36
April 5 - May 5	Yang Metal	Dragon	Yang Metal	Rat	April	55	2: 44
May 5 - June 6	Yin Metal	Snake	Yang Metal	Rat	May	25	20: 23
June 6 - July 7	Yang Water	Horse	Yang Metal	Rat	June	56	1: 11
July 7 - August 7	Yin Water	Sheep	Yang Metal	Rat	July	26	11: 13
August 7 - September 8	Yang Wood	Monkey	Yang Metal	Rat	Aug	57	21: 00
September 8 - October 8	Yin Wood	Cock	Yang Metal	Rat	Sep	28	: 39
October 8 - November 7	Yang Fire	Dog	Yang Metal	Rat	Oct	58	15: 09
November 7 - December 7	Yin Fire	Pig	Yang Metal	Rat	Nov	29	19: 06
December 7 - January 5	Yang Earth	Rat	Yang Metal	Rat	Dec	59	11: 26

1961

Find your Day Here	Month Stem	Branch	Year Stem	Branch	Day	Day	Time
January 5–February 4	Yin Earth	Ox	Yang Metal	Rat	Jan	30	21: 43
February 4–March 6	Yang Metal	Tiger	Yin Metal	Ox	Feb	1	9: 23
March 6–April 5	Yin Metal	Rabbit	Yin Metal	Ox	Mar	29	3: 35
April 5–May 6	Yang Water	Dragon	Yin Metal	Ox	April	60	8: 42
May 6–June 6	Yin Water	Snake	Yin Metal	Ox	May	30	2: 21
June 6–July 7	Yang Wood	Horse	Yin Metal	Ox	June	1	6: 46
July 7–August 8	Yin Wood	Sheep	Yin Metal	Ox	July	31	17: 07
August 8–September 8	Yang Fire	Monkey	Yin Metal	Ox	Aug	2	3: 27
September 8–October 8	Yin Fire	Cock	Yin Metal	Ox	Sep	33	5: 29
October 8–November 8	Yang Earth	Dog	Yin Metal	Ox	Oct	3	22: 03
November 8–December 7	Yin Earth	Pig	Yin Metal	Ox	Nov	34	: 55
December 7–January 6	Yang Metal	Rat	Yin Metal	Ox	Dec	4	17: 16

Branch	Pig	Rat	Ox	Tiger	Rabbit	Dragon	Snake	Horse	Sheep	Monkey	Cock	Dog
Main Element	Yang Water	Yin Water	Yin Earth	Yang Wood	Yin Wood	Yang Earth	Yang Fire	Yin Fire	Yin Earth	Yang Metal	Yin Metal	Yang Earth
Hidden Elements	Yang Wood		Yin Water	Yang Fire		Yin Wood	Yang Earth	Yin Earth	Yin Fire	Yang Earth		Yin Metal
			Yin Metal	Yang Earth		Yin Water	Yang Metal		Yin Wood	Yang Water		Yin Fire

1962

Find your Day Here	Month Stem	Branch	Year Stem	Branch	Day	Day	Time
January 6–February 4	Yin Metal	Ox	Yin Metal	Ox	Jan	35	3: 35
February 4–March 6	Yang Water	Tiger	Yang Water	Tiger	Feb	6	15: 18
March 6–April 5	Yin Water	Rabbit	Yang Water	Tiger	Mar	6	9: 30
April 5–May 6	Yang Wood	Dragon	Yang Water	Tiger	April	6	14: 34
May 6–June 6	Yin Wood	Snake	Yang Water	Tiger	May	35	8: 10
June 6–July 7	Yang Fire	Horse	Yang Water	Tiger	June	6	12: 31
July 7–August 8	Yin Fire	Sheep	Yang Water	Tiger	July	36	23: 16
August 8–September 8	Yang Earth	Monkey	Yang Water	Tiger	Aug	7	9: 34
September 8–October 9	Yin Earth	Cock	Yang Water	Tiger	Sep	38	11: 16
October 9–November 8	Yang Metal	Dog	Yang Water	Tiger	Oct	8	3: 57
November 8–December 7	Yin Metal	Pig	Yang Water	Tiger	Nov	39	5: 35
December 7–January 6	Yang Water	Rat	Yang Water	Tiger	Dec	9	23: 06

1963

Find your Day Here	Month Stem	Branch	Year Stem	Branch	Day	Day	Time
January 6–February 4	Yin Water	Ox	Yang Water	Tiger	Jan	40	9: 27
February 4–arch 6	Yang Wood	Tiger	Yin Water	Rabbit	Feb	11	21: 08
March 6–pril 5	Yin Wood	Rabbit	Yin Water	Rabbit	Mar	39	15: 17
April 5–May 6	Yang Fire	Dragon	Yin Water	Rabbit	April	10	20: 19
May 6–June 6	Yin Fire	Snake	Yin Water	Rabbit	May	40	13: 52
June 6–July 7	Yang Earth	Horse	Yin Water	Rabbit	June	11	18: 15
July 8–August 8	Yin Earth	Sheep	Yin Water	Rabbit	July	41	5: 05
August 8–September 8	Yang Metal	Monkey	Yin Water	Rabbit	Aug	12	15: 18
September 8–October 9	Yin Metal	Cock	Yin Water	Rabbit	Sep	43	17: 12
October 9–November 8	Yang Water	Dog	Yin Water	Rabbit	Oct	13	9: 41
November 8–December 8	Yin Water	Pig	Yin Water	Rabbit	Nov	44	11: 32
December 8–January 6	Yang Wood	Rat	Yin Water	Rabbit	Dec	14	4: 13

Branch	Pig	Rat	Ox	Tiger	Rabbit	Dragon	Snake	Horse	Sheep	Monkey	Cock	Dog
Main Element	Yang Water	Yin Water	Yin Earth	Yang Wood	Yin Wood	Yang Earth	Yang Fire	Yin Fire	Yin Earth	Yang Metal	Yin Metal	Yang Earth
Hidden Elements	Yang Wood		Yin Water	Yang Fire		Yin Wood	Yang Earth	Yin Earth	Yin Fire	Yang Earth		Yin Metal
			Yin Metal	Yang Earth		Yin Water	Yang Metal		Yin Wood	Yang Water		Yin Fire

1964

	Month		Year				
Find your Day Here	Stem	Branch	Stem	Branch	Day	Day	Time
January 6–February 5	Yin Wood	Ox	Yin Water	Rabbit	Jan	45	15: 22
February 5–29,–March 5	Yang Fire	Tiger	Yang Wood	Dragon	Feb	16	2: 56
March 5–April 5	Yin Fire	Rabbit	Yang Wood	Dragon	Mar	45	20: 58
April 5–May 5	Yang Earth	Dragon	Yang Wood	Dragon	April	16	2: 18
May 5–June 6	Yin Earth	Snake	Yang Wood	Dragon	May	46	19: 51
June 6–July 7	Yang Metal	Horse	Yang Wood	Dragon	June	17	: 12
July 7–August 7	Yin Metal	Sheep	Yang Wood	Dragon	July	47	10: 32
August 7–September 7	Yang Water	Monkey	Yang Wood	Dragon	Aug	18	20: 16
September 7–October 8	Yin Water	Cock	Yang Wood	Dragon	Sep	49	
October 8–November 7	Yang Wood	Dog	Yang Wood	Dragon	Oct	19	15: 30
November 7–December 7	Yin Wood	Pig	Yang Wood	Dragon	Nov	50	17: 15
December 7–January 5	Yang Fire	Rat	Yang Wood	Dragon	Dec	20	9: 53

1965

	Month		Year				
Find your Day Here	Stem	Branch	Stem	Branch	Day	Day	Time
January 5–February 4	Yin Fire	Ox	Yang Wood	Dragon	Jan	51	21: 02
February 4–arch 6	Yang Earth	Tiger	Yin Wood	Snake	Feb	27	8: 46
March 6–April 5	Yin Earth	Rabbit	Yin Wood	Snake	Mar	50	2: 48
April 5–May 6	Yang Metal	Dragon	Yin Wood	Snake	April	21	8: 07
May 6–June 6	Yin Metal	Snake	Yin Wood	Snake	May	51	1: 42
June 6–July 7	Yang Water	Horse	Yin Wood	Snake	June	22	6: 02
July 7–August 8	Yin Water	Sheep	Yin Wood	Snake	July	52	16: 22
August 8–September 8	Yang Wood	Monkey	Yin Wood	Snake	Aug	23	2: 05
September 8–October 8	Yin Wood	Cock	Yin Wood	Snake	Sep	54	5: 41
October 8–November 7	Yang Fire	Dog	Yin Wood	Snake	Oct	24	21: 19
November 7–December 7	Yin Fire	Pig	Yin Wood	Snake	Nov	55	: 13
December 7–January 6	Yang Earth	Rat	Yin Wood	Snake	Dec	25	15: 46

Branch	Pig	Rat	Ox	Tiger	Rabbit	Dragon	Snake	Horse	Sheep	Monkey	Cock	Dog
Main Element	Yang Water	Yin Water	Yin Earth	Yang Wood	Yin Wood	Yang Earth	Yang Fire	Yin Fire	Yin Earth	Yang Metal	Yin Metal	Yang Earth
Hidden Elements	Yang Wood		Yin Water	Yang Fire		Yin Wood	Yang Earth	Yin Earth	Yin Fire	Yang Earth		Yin Metal
			Yin Metal	Yang Earth		Yin Water	Yang Metal		Yin Wood	Yang Water		Yin Fire

1966

Find your Day Here	Month Stem	Branch	Year Stem	Branch	Day	Day	Time
January 6–February 4	Yin Earth	Ox	Yin Wood	Snake	Jan	56	3:16
February 4–29, March 6	Yang Metal	Tiger	Yang Fire	Horse	Feb	27	14:38
March 6–April 5	Yin Metal	Rabbit	Yang Fire	Horse	Mar	55	8:51
April 5–May 6	Yang Water	Dragon	Yang Fire	Horse	April	26	13:57
May 6–June 6	Yin Water	Snake	Yang Fire	Horse	May	56	7:31
June 6–July 7	Yang Wood	Horse	Yang Fire	Horse	June	27	11:50
July 7–August 8	Yin Wood	Sheep	Yang Fire	Horse	July	57	22:07
August 8–September 8	Yang Fire	Monkey	Yang Fire	Horse	Aug	28	7:49
September 8–October 9	Yin Fire	Cock	Yang Fire	Horse	Sep	59	11:30
October 9–November 8	Yang Earth	Dog	Yang Fire	Horse	Oct	29	3:08
November 8–December 7	Yin Earth	Pig	Yang Fire	Horse	Nov	60	6:02
December 7–January 6	Yang Metal	Rat	Yang Fire	Horse	Dec	30	21:38

1967

Find your Day Here	Month Stem	Branch	Year Stem	Branch	Day	Day	Time
January 6–February 4	Yin Metal	Ox	Yang Fire	Horse	Jan	1	9:06
February 4–March 6	Yang Water	Tiger	Yin Fire	Sheep	Feb	32	20:31
March 6–April 5	Yin Water	Rabbit	Yin Fire	Sheep	Mar	60	14:42
April 5–May 6	Yang Wood	Dragon	Yin Fire	Sheep	April	31	19:42
May 6–June 6	Yin Wood	Snake	Yin Fire	Sheep	May	1	13:18
June 6–July 8	Yang Fire	Horse	Yin Fire	Sheep	June	32	17:36
July 8–August 8	Yin Fire	Sheep	Yin Fire	Sheep	July	2	3:54
August 8–September 8	Yang Earth	Monkey	Yin Fire	Sheep	Aug	33	13:35
September 8–October 9	Yin Earth	Cock	Yin Fire	Sheep	Sep	4	17:18
October 9–November 8	Yang Metal	Dog	Yin Fire	Sheep	Oct	34	7:42
November 8–December 8	Yin Metal	Pig	Yin Fire	Sheep	Nov	5	11:52
December 8–January 6	Yang Water	Rat	Yin Fire	Sheep	Dec	35	3:18

Branch	Pig	Rat	Ox	Tiger	Rabbit	Dragon	Snake	Horse	Sheep	Monkey	Cock	Dog
Main Element	Yang Water	Yin Water	Yin Earth	Yang Wood	Yin Wood	Yang Earth	Yang Fire	Yin Fire	Yin Earth	Yang Metal	Yin Metal	Yang Earth
Hidden Elements	Yang Wood		Yin Water	Yang Fire		Yin Wood	Yang Earth	Yin Earth	Yin Fire	Yang Earth		Yin Metal
			Yin Metal	Yang Earth		Yin Water	Yang Metal		Yin Wood	Yang Water		Yin Fire

1968

	Month		Year				
Find your Day Here	Stem	Branch	Stem	Branch	Day	Day	Time
January 6–February 5	Yin Water	Ox	Yin Fire	Sheep	Jan	6	14: 26
February 5–29,–March 5	Yang Wood	Tiger	Yang Earth	Monkey	Feb	37	2: 08
March 5–April 5	Yin Wood	Rabbit	Yang Earth	Monkey	Mar	6	20: 18
April 5–May 5	Yang Fire	Dragon	Yang Earth	Monkey	April	37	1: 21
May 5–June 6	Yin Fire	Snake	Yang Earth	Monkey	May	7	19: 50
June 6–July 7	Yang Earth	Horse	Yang Earth	Monkey	June	38	23: 19
July 7–August 7	Yin Earth	Sheep	Yang Earth	Monkey	July	8	9: 42
August 7–September 7	Yang Metal	Monkey	Yang Earth	Monkey	Aug	39	19: 27
September 7–October 8	Yin Metal	Cock	Yang Earth	Monkey	Sep	10	23: 07
October 8–November 7	Yang Water	Dog	Yang Earth	Monkey	Oct	40	13: 35
November 7–December 7	Yin Water	Pig	Yang Earth	Monkey	Nov	11	17: 41
December 7–January 5	Yang Wood	Rat	Yang Earth	Monkey	Dec	41	9: 09

1969

	Month		Year				
Find your Day Here	Stem	Branch	Stem	Branch	Day	Day	Time
January 5–February 4	Yin Wood	Ox	Yang Earth	Monkey	Jan	12	20: 17
February 4–March 6	Yang Fire	Tiger	Yin Earth	Cock	Feb	43	7: 59
March 6–April 5	Yin Fire	Rabbit	Yin Earth	Cock	Mar	11	2: 11
April 5–May 6	Yang Earth	Dragon	Yin Earth	Cock	April	42	7: 15
May 6–June 6	Yin Earth	Snake	Yin Earth	Cock	May	12	: 50
June 6–July 7	Yang Metal	Horse	Yin Earth	Cock	June	43	5: 12
July 7–August 8	Yin Metal	Sheep	Yin Earth	Cock	July	13	15: 32
August 8–September 8	Yang Water	Monkey	Yin Earth	Cock	Aug	44	1: 14
September 8–October 8	Yin Water	Cock	Yin Earth	Cock	Sep	15	3: 56
October 8–November 7	Yang Wood	Dog	Yin Earth	Cock	Oct	45	19: 17
November 7–December 7	Yin Wood	Pig	Yin Earth	Cock	Nov	16	23: 31
December 7–January 6	Yang Fire	Rat	Yin Earth	Cock	Dec	46	15: 54

Branch	Pig	Rat	Ox	Tiger	Rabbit	Dragon	Snake	Horse	Sheep	Monkey	Cock	Dog
Main Element	Yang Water	Yin Water	Yin Earth	Yang Wood	Yin Wood	Yang Earth	Yang Fire	Yin Fire	Yin Earth	Yang Metal	Yin Metal	Yang Earth
Hidden Elements	Yang Wood		Yin Water	Yang Fire		Yin Wood	Yang Earth	Yin Earth	Yin Fire	Yang Earth		Yin Metal
			Yin Metal	Yang Earth		Yin Water	Yang Metal		Yin Wood	Yang Water		Yin Fire

1970

Find your Day Here	Month Stem	Branch	Year Stem	Branch	Day	Day	Time
January 6–February 4	Yin Fire	Ox	Yin Earth	Cock	Jan	17	1:59
February 4–March 6	Yang Earth	Tiger	Yang Metal	Dog	Feb	48	13:46
March 6–April 5	Yin Earth	Rabbit	Yang Metal	Dog	Mar	16	7:51
April 5–May 6	Yang Metal	Dragon	Yang Metal	Dog	April	47	13:00
May 6–June 6	Yin Metal	Snake	Yang Metal	Dog	May	17	6:28
June 6–July 7	Yang Water	Horse	Yang Metal	Dog	June	48	11:13
July 7–August 8	Yin Water	Sheep	Yang Metal	Dog	July	18	21:14
August 8–September 8	Yang Wood	Monkey	Yang Metal	Dog	Aug	49	7:20
September 8–October 9	Yin Wood	Cock	Yang Metal	Dog	Sep	20	9:42
October 9–November 8	Yang Fire	Dog	Yang Metal	Dog	Oct	50	1:06
November 8–December 7	Yin Fire	Pig	Yang Metal	Dog	Nov	21	5:20
December 7–January 6	Yang Earth	Rat	Yang Metal	Dog	Dec	51	21:43

1971

Find your Day Here	Month Stem	Branch	Year Stem	Branch	Day	Day	Time
January 6–February 4	Yin Earth	Ox	Yang Metal	Dog	Jan	22	7: 45
February 4–29, March 6	Yang Metal	Tiger	Yin Metal	Pig	Feb	53	19 :26
March 6–April 5	Yin Metal	Rabbit	Yin Metal	Pig	Mar	21	13: 35
April 5–May 6	Yang Water	Dragon	Yin Metal	Pig	April	52	18: 36
May 6–June 6	Yin Water	Snake	Yin Metal	Pig	May	22	12: 08
June 6–July 8	Yang Wood	Horse	Yin Metal	Pig	June	53	17: 00
July 8–August 8	Yin Wood	Sheep	Yin Metal	Pig	July	23	3:29
August 8–September 8	Yang Fire	Monkey	Yin Metal	Pig	Aug	54	13: 29
September 8–October 9	Yin Fire	Cock	Yin Metal	Pig	Sep	25	17: 30
October 9–November 8	Yang Earth	Dog	Yin Metal	Pig	Oct	55	8: 13
November 8–December 8	Yin Earth	Pig	Yin Metal	Pig	Nov	26	11: 10
December 8–January 6	Yang Metal	Rat	Yin Metal	Pig	Dec	56	3: 33

Branch	Pig	Rat	Ox	Tiger	Rabbit	Dragon	Snake	Horse	Sheep	Monkey	Cock	Dog
Main Element	Yang Water	Yin Water	Yin Earth	Yang Wood	Yin Wood	Yang Earth	Yang Fire	Yin Fire	Yin Earth	Yang Metal	Yin Metal	Yang Earth
Hidden Elements	Yang Wood		Yin Water	Yang Fire		Yin Wood	Yang Earth	Yin Earth	Yin Fire	Yang Earth		Yin Metal
			Yin Metal	Yang Earth		Yin Water	Yang Metal		Yin Wood	Yang Water		Yin Fire

1972

| | Month | | Year | | | | |
Find your Day Here	Stem	Branch	Stem	Branch	Day	Day	Time
January 6–February 5	Yin Metal	Ox	Yin Metal	Pig	Jan	27	13:43
February 5–29,–March 5	Yang Water	Tiger	Yang Water	Rat	Feb	58	1:20
March 5–April 5	Yin Water	Rabbit	Yang Water	Rat	Mar	27	19:28
April 5–May 5	Yang Wood	Dragon	Yang Water	Rat	April	58	:36
May 5–June 5	Yin Wood	Snake	Yang Water	Rat	May	59	18:26
June 5–July 7	Yang Fire	Horse	Yang Water	Rat	June	59	22:22
July 7–August 7	Yin Fire	Sheep	Yang Water	Rat	July	29	9:17
August 7–September 7	Yang Earth	Monkey	Yang Water	Rat	Aug	31	19:17
September 7–October 8	Yin Earth	Cock	Yang Water	Rat	Sep	31	21:15
October 8–November 7	Yang Metal	Dog	Yang Water	Rat	Oct	1	14:02
November 7–December 7	Yin Metal	Pig	Yang Water	Rat	Nov	32	15:40
December 7–January 5	Yang Water	Rat	Yang Water	Rat	Dec	2	9:23

1973

| | Month | | Year | | | | |
Find your Day Here	Stem	Branch	Stem	Branch	Day	Day	Time
January 5–February 4	Yin Water	Ox	Yang Water	Rat	Jan	33	19:26
February 4–March 6	Yang Wood	Tiger	Yin Water	Ox	Feb	4	7:04
March 6–April 5	Yin Wood	Rabbit	Yin Water	Ox	Mar	32	1:13
April 5–May 6	Yang Fire	Dragon	Yin Water	Ox	April	3	6:14
May 6–June 6	Yin Fire	Snake	Yin Water	Ox	May	33	:08
June 6–July 7	Yang Earth	Horse	Yin Water	Ox	June	4	4:07
July 7–August 8	Yin Earth	Sheep	Yin Water	Ox	July	34	15:05
August 8–September 8	Yang Metal	Monkey	Yin Water	Ox	Aug	5	1:05
September 8–October 8	Yin Metal	Cock	Yin Water	Ox	Sep	36	3:00
October 8–November 7	Yang Water	Dog	Yin Water	Ox	Oct	6	22:48
November 7–December 7	Yin Water	Pig	Yin Water	Ox	Nov	37	21:28
December 7–January 6	Yang Wood	Rat	Yin Water	Ox	Dec	7	15:13

Branch	Pig	Rat	Ox	Tiger	Rabbit	Dragon	Snake	Horse	Sheep	Monkey	Cock	Dog
Main Element	Yang Water	Yin Water	Yin Earth	Yang Wood	Yin Wood	Yang Earth	Yang Fire	Yin Fire	Yin Earth	Yang Metal	Yin Metal	Yang Earth
Hidden Elements	Yang Wood		Yin Water	Yang Fire		Yin Wood	Yang Earth	Yin Earth	Yin Fire	Yang Earth		Yin Metal
			Yin Metal	Yang Earth		Yin Water	Yang Metal		Yin Wood	Yang Water		Yin Fire

1974

Find your Day Here	Month Stem	Branch	Year Stem	Branch	Day	Day	Time
January 6–February 4	Yin Wood	Ox	Yin Water	Ox	Jan	38	1:20
February 4–March 6	Yang Fire	Tiger	Yang Wood	Tiger	Feb	9	13:00
March 6–April 5	Yin Fire	Rabbit	Yang Wood	Tiger	Mar	37	7:07
April 5–May 6	Yang Earth	Dragon	Yang Wood	Tiger	April	8	12:05
May 6–June 6	Yin Earth	Snake	Yang Wood	Tiger	May	38	5:34
June 6–July 7	Yang Metal	Horse	Yang Wood	Tiger	June	9	9:52
July 7–August 8	Yin Metal	Sheep	Yang Wood	Tiger	July	39	20:13
August 8–September 8	Yang Water	Monkey	Yang Wood	Tiger	Aug	10	5:57
September 8–October 9	Yin Water	Cock	Yang Wood	Tiger	Sep	41	9:58
October 9–November 8	Yang Wood	Dog	Yang Wood	Tiger	Oct	11	1:40
November 8–December 7	Yin Wood	Pig	Yang Wood	Tiger	Nov	42	3:18
December 7–January 6	Yang Fire	Rat	Yang Wood	Tiger	Dec	12	21:02

1975

Find your Day Here	Month Stem	Branch	Year Stem	Branch	Day	Day	Time
January 6–February 4	Yin Fire	Ox	Yang Wood	Tiger	Jan	43	:36
February 4–March 6	Yang Earth	Tiger	Yin Wood	Rabbit	Feb	14	19:02
March 6–April 5	Yin Earth	Rabbit	Yin Wood	Rabbit	Mar	42	13:07
April 5–May 6	Yang Metal	Dragon	Yin Wood	Rabbit	April	13	18:02
May 6–June 6	Yin Metal	Snake	Yin Wood	Rabbit	May	43	11:27
June 6–July 8	Yang Water	Horse	Yin Wood	Rabbit	June	14	15:42
July 8–August 8	Yin Water	Sheep	Yin Wood	Rabbit	July	44	2:00
August 8–September 8	Yang Wood	Monkey	Yin Wood	Rabbit	Aug	15	11:45
September 8–October 9	Yin Wood	Cock	Yin Wood	Rabbit	Sep	46	15:47
October 9–November 8	Yang Fire	Dog	Yin Wood	Rabbit	Oct	16	7:29
November 8–December 8	Yin Fire	Pig	Yin Wood	Rabbit	Nov	47	9:03
December 8–January 6	Yang Earth	Rat	Yin Wood	Rabbit	Dec	17	1:46

Branch	Pig	Rat	Ox	Tiger	Rabbit	Dragon	Snake	Horse	Sheep	Monkey	Cock	Dog
Main Element	Yang Water	Yin Water	Yin Earth	Yang Wood	Yin Wood	Yang Earth	Yang Fire	Yang Fire	Yin Earth	Yang Metal	Yin Metal	Yang Earth
Hidden Elements	Yang Wood		Yin Water	Yang Fire		Yin Wood	Yang Earth	Yin Earth	Yin Fire	Yang Earth		Yin Metal
			Yin Metal	Yang Earth		Yin Water	Yang Metal		Yin Wood	Yang Water		Yin Fire

1976

Find your Day Here	Month Stem	Branch	Year Stem	Branch	Day	Day	Time
January 6–February 5	Yin Earth	Ox	Yin Wood	Rabbit	Jan	48	13:43
February 5–29,–March 5	Yang Metal	Tiger	Yang Fire	Dragon	Feb	19	:40
March 5–April 5	Yin Metal	Rabbit	Yang Fire	Dragon	Mar	48	18:48
April 5–May 5	Yang Water	Dragon	Yang Fire	Dragon	April	19	23:47
May 5–June 5	Yin Water	Snake	Yang Fire	Dragon	May	49	17:15
June 5–July 7	Yang Wood	Horse	Yang Fire	Dragon	June	20	21:31
July 7–August 7	Yin Wood	Sheep	Yang Fire	Dragon	July	50	7:51
August 7–September 7	Yang Fire	Monkey	Yang Fire	Dragon	Aug	21	17:38
September 7–October 8	Yin Fire	Cock	Yang Fire	Dragon	Sep	52	21:36
October 8–November 7	Yang Earth	Dog	Yang Fire	Dragon	Oct	22	13:18
November 7–December 7	Yin Earth	Pig	Yang Fire	Dragon	Nov	53	16:17
December 7–January 5	Yang Metal	Rat	Yang Fire	Dragon	Dec	23	7:41

1977

Find your Day Here	Month Stem	Branch	Year Stem	Branch	Day	Day	Time
January 5–February 4	Yin Metal	Ox	Yang Fire	Dragon	Jan	54	19:24
February 4–March 6	Yang Water	Tiger	Yin Fire	Snake	Feb	25	6:34
March 6–April 5	Yin Water	Rabbit	Yin Fire	Snake	Mar	53	:44
April 5–May 6	Yang Wood	Dragon	Yin Fire	Snake	April	24	5:40
May 6–June 6	Yin Wood	Snake	Yin Fire	Snake	May	54	23:16
June 6–July 7	Yang Fire	Horse	Yin Fire	Snake	June	25	3:23
July 7–August 8	Yin Fire	Sheep	Yin Fire	Snake	July	55	13:48
August 8–September 8	Yang Earth	Monkey	Yin Fire	Snake	Aug	26	:18
September 8–October 8	Yin Earth	Cock	Yin Fire	Snake	Sep	57	3:24
October 8–November 7	Yang Metal	Dog	Yin Fire	Snake	Oct	27	19:07
November 7–December 7	Yin Metal	Pig	Yin Fire	Snake	Nov	58	22:06
December 7–January 6	Yang Water	Rat	Yin Fire	Snake	Dec	28	13:31

Branch	Pig	Rat	Ox	Tiger	Rabbit	Dragon	Snake	Horse	Sheep	Monkey	Cock	Dog
Main Element	Yang Water	Yin Water	Yin Earth	Yang Wood	Yin Wood	Yang Earth	Yang Fire	Yin Fire	Yin Earth	Yang Metal	Yin Metal	Yang Earth
Hidden Elements	Yang Wood		Yin Water	Yang Fire		Yin Wood	Yang Earth	Yin Earth	Yin Fire	Yang Earth		Yin Metal
			Yin Metal	Yang Earth		Yin Water	Yang Metal		Yin Wood	Yang Water		Yin Fire

1978

Find your Day Here	Month Stem	Branch	Year Stem	Branch	Day	Day	Time
January 6–February 4	Yin Water	Ox	Yin Fire	Snake	Jan	59	1:13
February 4–March 6	Yang Wood	Tiger	Yang Earth	Horse	Feb	30	12:27
March 6–April 5	Yin Wood	Rabbit	Yang Earth	Horse	Mar	58	6:38
April 5–May 6	Yang Fire	Dragon	Yang Earth	Horse	April	29	11:39
May 6–June 6	Yin Fire	Snake	Yang Earth	Horse	May	59	5:09
June 6–July 7	Yang Earth	Horse	Yang Earth	Horse	June	30	9:23
July 7–August 8	Yin Earth	Sheep	Yang Earth	Horse	July	60	19:37
August 8–September 8	Yang Metal	Monkey	Yang Earth	Horse	Aug	31	5:18
September 8–October 9	Yin Metal	Cock	Yang Earth	Horse	Sep	2	8:08
October 9–November 8	Yang Water	Dog	Yang Earth	Horse	Oct	32	23:31
November 8–December 7	Yin Water	Pig	Yang Earth	Horse	Nov	3	2:34
December 7–January 6	Yang Wood	Rat	Yang Earth	Horse	Dec	33	19:20

1979

Find your Day Here	Month Stem	Branch	Year Stem	Branch	Day	Day	Time
January 6–February 4	Yin Wood	Ox	Yang Earth	Horse	Jan	4	6:32
February 4–March 6	Yang Fire	Tiger	Yin Earth	Sheep	Feb	35	18:13
March 6–April 5	Yin Fire	Rabbit	Yin Earth	Sheep	Mar	3	12:20
April 5–May 6	Yang Earth	Dragon	Yin Earth	Sheep	April	34	17:18
May 6–June 6	Yin Earth	Snake	Yin Earth	Sheep	May	4	10:47
June 6–July 8	Yang Metal	Horse	Yin Earth	Sheep	June	35	15:05
July 8–August 8	Yin Metal	Sheep	Yin Earth	Sheep	July	5	1:25
August 8–September 8	Yang Water	Monkey	Yin Earth	Sheep	Aug	36	11:11
September 8–October 9	Yin Water	Cock	Yin Earth	Sheep	Sep	7	15:01
October 9–November 8	Yang Wood	Dog	Yin Earth	Sheep	Oct	37	5:30
November 8–December 8	Yin Wood	Pig	Yin Earth	Sheep	Nov	8	9:45
December 8–January 6	Yang Fire	Rat	Yin Earth	Sheep	Dec	38	1:18

Branch	Pig	Rat	Ox	Tiger	Rabbit	Dragon	Snake	Horse	Sheep	Monkey	Cock	Dog
Main Element	Yang Water	Yin Water	Yin Earth	Yang Wood	Yin Wood	Yang Earth	Yang Fire	Yin Fire	Yin Earth	Yang Metal	Yin Metal	Yang Earth
Hidden Elements	Yang Wood		Yin Water	Yang Fire		Yin Wood	Yang Earth	Yin Earth	Yin Fire	Yang Earth		Yin Metal
			Yin Metal	Yang Earth		Yin Water	Yang Metal		Yin Wood	Yang Water		Yin Fire

1980

| | Month | | Year | | | | |
Find your Day Here	Stem	Branch	Stem	Branch	Day	Day	Time
January 6–February 5	Yin Fire	Ox	Yin Earth	Sheep	Jan	9	12: 29
February 5–29,–March 5	Yang Earth	Tiger	Yang Metal	Monkey	Feb	40	: 10
March 5–April 4	Yin Earth	Rabbit	Yang Metal	Monkey	Mar	9	18: 17
April 4–May 5	Yang Metal	Dragon	Yang Metal	Monkey	April	40	23: 15
May 5–June 5	Yin Metal	Snake	Yang Metal	Monkey	May	10	16: 45
June 5–July 7	Yang Water	Horse	Yang Metal	Monkey	June	41	21: 14
July 7–August 7	Yin Water	Sheep	Yang Metal	Monkey	July	11	7; 24
August 7–September 7	Yang Wood	Monkey	Yang Metal	Monkey	Aug	42	17: 09
September 7–October 8	Yin Wood	Cock	Yang Metal	Monkey	Sep	13	19: 54
October 8–November 7	Yang Fire	Dog	Yang Metal	Monkey	Oct	43	11: 20
November 7–December 7	Yin Fire	Pig	Yang Metal	Monkey	Nov	14	15: 35
December 7–January 5	Yang Earth	Rat	Yang Metal	Monkey	Dec	44	7: 02

1981

| | Month | | Year | | | | |
Find your Day Here	Stem	Branch	Stem	Branch	Day	Day	Time
January 5–February 4	Yin Earth	Ox	Yang Metal	Monkey	Jan	15	18: 13
February 4–March 6	Yang Metal	Tiger	Yin Metal	Cock	Feb	46	5: 56
March 6–April 5	Yin Metal	Rabbit	Yin Metal	Cock	Mar	14	23: 58
April 5–May 5	Yang Water	Dragon	Yin Metal	Cock	April	45	4: 59
May 5–June 6	Yin Water	Snake	Yin Metal	Cock	May	15	22: 35
June 6–July 7	Yang Wood	Horse	Yin Metal	Cock	June	46	3: 03
July 7–August 7	Yin Wood	Sheep	Yin Metal	Cock	July	16	13: 12
August 7–September 8	Yang Fire	Monkey	Yin Metal	Cock	Aug	47	23: 31
September 8–October 8	Yin Fire	Cock	Yin Metal	Cock	Sep	18	1: 43
October 8–November 7	Yang Earth	Dog	Yin Metal	Cock	Oct	48	17: 10
November 7–December 7	Yin Earth	Pig	Yin Metal	Cock	Nov	19	21: 24
December 7–January 6	Yang Metal	Rat	Yin Metal	Cock	Dec	49	13: 51

Branch	Pig	Rat	Ox	Tiger	Rabbit	Dragon	Snake	Horse	Sheep	Monkey	Cock	Dog
Main Element	Yang Water	Yin Water	Yin Earth	Yang Wood	Yin Wood	Yang Earth	Yang Fire	Yin Fire	Yin Earth	Yang Metal	Yin Metal	Yang Earth
Hidden Elements	Yang Wood		Yin Water	Yang Fire		Yin Wood	Yang Earth	Yin Earth	Yin Fire	Yang Earth		Yin Metal
			Yin Metal	Yang Earth		Yin Water	Yang Metal		Yin Wood	Yang Water		Yin Fire

1982

Find your Day Here	Month Stem	Branch	Year Stem	Branch	Day	Day	Time
January 6–February 4	Yin Metal	Ox	Yin Metal	Cock	Jan	20	: 02
February 4–March 6	Yang Water	Tiger	Yang Water	Dog	Feb	51	11: 46
March 6–April 5	Yin Water	Rabbit	Yang Water	Dog	Mar	19	5: 57
April 5–May 6	Yang Wood	Dragon	Yang Water	Dog	April	50	10: 54
May 6–June 6	Yin Wood	Snake	Yang Water	Dog	May	20	4: 21
June 6–July 7	Yang Fire	Horse	Yang Water	Dog	June	51	8: 36
July 7–August 8	Yin Fire	Sheep	Yang Water	Dog	July	21	19: 19
August 8–September 8	Yang Earth	Monkey	Yang Water	Dog	Aug	52	5: 19
September 8–October 8	Yin Earth	Cock	Yang Water	Dog	Sep	23	7: 32
October 8–November 8	Yang Metal	Dog	Yang Water	Dog	Oct	53	: 12
November 8–December 7	Yin Metal	Pig	Yang Water	Dog	Nov	24	3: 13
December 7–January 6	Yang Water	Rat	Yang Water	Dog	Dec	54	19: 40

1983

Find your Day Here	Month Stem	Branch	Year Stem	Branch	Day	Day	Time
January 6–February 4	Yin Water	Ox	Yang Water	Dog	Jan	25	5: 49
February 4–March 6	Yang Wood	Tiger	Yin Water	Pig	Feb	56	17: 40
March 6–April 5	Yin Wood	Rabbit	Yin Water	Pig	Mar	24	11: 48
April 5–May 6	Yang Fire	Dragon	Yin Water	Pig	April	55	16: 45
May 6–June 6	Yin Fire	Snake	Yin Water	Pig	May	25	10: 12
June 6–July 8	Yang Earth	Horse	Yin Water	Pig	June	56	14: 27
July 8–August 8	Yin Earth	Sheep	Yin Water	Pig	July	26	1: 06
August 8–September 8	Yang Metal	Monkey	Yin Water	Pig	Aug	57	11: 07
September 8–October 9	Yin Metal	Cock	Yin Water	Pig	Sep	28	13: 21
October 9–November 8	Yang Water	Dog	Yin Water	Pig	Oct	58	6: 01
November 8–December 8	Yin Water	Pig	Yin Water	Pig	Nov	29	9: 03
December 8–January 6	Yang Wood	Rat	Yin Water	Pig	Dec	59	1: 30

Branch	Pig	Rat	Ox	Tiger	Rabbit	Dragon	Snake	Horse	Sheep	Monkey	Cock	Dog
Main Element	Yang Water	Yin Water	Yin Earth	Yang Wood	Yin Wood	Yang Earth	Yang Fire	Yin Fire	Yin Earth	Yang Metal	Yin Metal	Yang Earth
Hidden Elements	Yang Wood		Yin Water	Yang Fire		Yin Wood	Yang Earth	Yin Earth	Yin Fire	Yang Earth		Yin Metal
			Yin Metal	Yang Earth		Yin Water	Yang Metal		Yin Wood	Yang Water		Yin Fire

1984

Find your Day Here	Month Stem	Branch	Year Stem	Branch	Day	Day	Time
January 6–February 5	Yin Wood	Ox	Yin Water	Pig	Jan	30	11:42
February 5–29,–March 5	Yang Fire	Tiger	Yang Wood	Rat	Feb	1	23:19
March 5–April 4	Yin Fire	Rabbit	Yang Wood	Rat	Mar	30	17:25
April 4–May 5	Yang Earth	Dragon	Yang Wood	Rat	April	1	22:23
May 5–June 5	Yin Earth	Snake	Yang Wood	Rat	May	31	15:51
June 5–July 7	Yang Metal	Horse	Yang Wood	Rat	June	2	20:09
July 7–August 7	Yin Metal	Sheep	Yang Wood	Rat	July	32	6:29
August 7–September 7	Yang Water	Monkey	Yang Wood	Rat	Aug	3	16:18
September 7–October 8	Yin Water	Cock	Yang Wood	Rat	Sep	34	19:10
October 8–November 7	Yang Wood	Dog	Yang Wood	Rat	Oct	4	11:50
November 7–December 7	Yin Wood	Pig	Yang Wood	Rat	Nov	35	13:46
December 7–January 5	Yang Fire	Rat	Yang Wood	Rat	Dec	5	7:20

1985

Find your Day Here	Month Stem	Branch	Year Stem	Branch	Day	Day	Time
January 5–February 4	Yin Fire	Ox	Yang Wood	Rat	Jan	36	18:36
February 4–March 5	Yang Earth	Tiger	Yin Wood	Ox	Feb	7	6:12
March 5–April 5	Yin Earth	Rabbit	Yin Wood	Ox	Mar	35	23:16
April 5–May 5	Yang Metal	Dragon	Yin Wood	· Ox	April	6	4:14
May 5–June 6	Yin Metal	Snake	Yin Wood	Ox	May	36	21:43
June 6–July 7	Yang Water	Horse	Yin Wood	Ox	June	7	2:00
July 7–August 7	Yin Water	Sheep	Yin Wood	Ox	July	37	12:19
August 7–September 7	Yang Wood	Monkey	Yin Wood	Ox	Aug	8	22:04
September 8–October 8	Yin Wood	Cock	Yin Wood	Ox	Sep	39	1:53
October 8–November 7	Yang Fire	Dog	Yin Wood	Ox	Oct	9	17:39
November 7–December 7	Yin Fire	Pig	Yin Wood	Ox	Nov	40	19:29
December 7–January 5	Yang Earth	Rat	Yin Wood	Ox	Dec	10	13:09

Branch	Pig	Rat	Ox	Tiger	Rabbit	Dragon	Snake	Horse	Sheep	Monkey	Cock	Dog
Main Element	Yang Water	Yin Water	Yin Earth	Yang Wood	Yin Wood	Yang Earth	Yang Fire	Yin Fire	Yin Earth	Yang Metal	Yin Metal	Yang Earth
Hidden Elements	Yang Wood		Yin Water	Yang Fire		Yin Wood	Yang Earth	Yin Earth	Yin Fire	Yang Earth		Yin Metal
			Yin Metal	Yang Earth		Yin Water	Yang Metal		Yin Wood	Yang Water		Yin Fire

1986

Find your Day Here	Month Stem	Branch	Year Stem	Branch	Day	Day	Time
January 5–February 4	Yin Earth	Ox	Yin Wood	Ox	Jan	41	23:21
February 4–March 6	Yang Metal	Tiger	Yang Fire	Tiger	Feb	12	11:03
March 6–April 6	Yin Metal	Rabbit	Yang Fire	Tiger	Mar	40	5:13
April 6–May 6	Yang Water	Dragon	Yang Fire	Tiger	April	11	10:16
May 6–June 6	Yin Water	Snake	Yang Fire	Tiger	May	41	3:50
June 6–July 7	Yang Wood	Horse	Yang Fire	Tiger	June	12	8:12
July 7–August 8	Yin Wood	Sheep	Yang Fire	Tiger	July	42	18:35
August 8–September 8	Yang Fire	Monkey	Yang Fire	Tiger	Aug	13	4:17
September 8–October 8	Yin Fire	Cock	Yang Fire	Tiger	Sep	44	7:10
October 8–November 8	Yang Earth	Dog	Yang Fire	Tiger	Oct	14	23:28
November 8–December 7	Yin Earth	Pig	Yang Fire	Tiger	Nov	45	1:20
December 7–January 6	Yang Metal	Rat	Yang Fire	Tiger	Dec	15	18:01

1987

Find your Day Here	Month Stem	Branch	Year Stem	Branch	Day	Day	Time
January 6–February 4	Yin Metal	Ox	Yang Fire	Tiger	Jan	46	5:09
February 4–March 6	Yang Water	Tiger	Yin Fire	Rabbit	Feb	22	16:50
March 6–April 5	Yin Water	Rabbit	Yin Fire	Rabbit	Mar	45	10:59
April 5–May 6	Yang Wood	Dragon	Yin Fire	Rabbit	April	16	16:03
May 6–June 6	Yin Wood	Snake	Yin Fire	Rabbit	May	46	9:37
June 6–July 8	Yang Fire	Horse	Yin Fire	Rabbit	June	17	13:59
July 8–August 8	Yin Fire	Sheep	Yin Fire	Rabbit	July	47	:22
August 8–September 8	Yang Earth	Monkey	Yin Fire	Rabbit	Aug	18	10:04
September 8–October 9	Yin Earth	Cock	Yin Fire	Rabbit	Sep	49	13:33
October 9–November 8	Yang Metal	Dog	Yin Fire	Rabbit	Oct	19	5:17
November 8–December 8	Yin Metal	Pig	Yin Fire	Rabbit	Nov	50	7:07
December 8–January 6	Yang Water	Rat	Yin Fire	Rabbit	Dec	20	:49

Branch	Pig	Rat	Ox	Tiger	Rabbit	Dragon	Snake	Horse	Sheep	Monkey	Cock	Dog
Main Element	Yang Water	Yin Water	Yin Earth	Yang Wood	Yin Wood	Yang Earth	Yang Fire	Yin Fire	Yin Earth	Yang Metal	Yin Metal	Yang Earth
Hidden Elements	Yang Wood		Yin Water	Yang Fire		Yin Wood	Yang Earth	Yin Earth	Yin Fire	Yang Earth		Yin Metal
			Yin Metal	Yang Earth		Yin Water	Yang Metal		Yin Wood	Yang Water		Yin Fire

1988

	Month		Year				
Find your Day Here	Stem	Branch	Stem	Branch	Day	Day	Time
January 6–February 4	Yin Water	Ox	Yin Fire	Rabbit	Jan	51	11: 32
February 4–29,–March 5	Yang Wood	Tiger	Yang Earth	Dragon	Feb	22	22: 38
March 5–April 4	Yin Wood	Rabbit	Yang Earth	Dragon	Mar	51	16: 48
April 4–May 5	Yang Fire	Dragon	Yang Earth	Dragon	April	22	21: 51
May 5–June 5	Yin Fire	Snake	Yang Earth	Dragon	May	52	15: 25
June 5–July 7	Yang Earth	Horse	Yang Earth	Dragon	June	23	19: 47
July 7–August 7	Yin Earth	Sheep	Yang Earth	Dragon	July	53	6: 10
August 7–September 7	Yang Metal	Monkey	Yang Earth	Dragon	Aug	24	15: 52
September 7–October 8	Yin Metal	Cock	Yang Earth	Dragon	Sep	55	19: 18
October 8–November 7	Yang Water	Dog	Yang Earth	Dragon	Oct	25	11: 06
November 7–ecember 7	Yin Water	Pig	Yang Earth	Dragon	Nov	56	14: 10
December 7–January 5	Yang Wood	Rat	Yang Earth	Dragon	Dec	26	5: 35

1989

	Month		Year				
Find your Day Here	Stem	Branch	Stem	Branch	Day	Day	Time
January 5–February 4	Yin Wood	Ox	Yang Earth	Dragon	Jan	57	17:21
February 4–March 5	Yang Fire	Tiger	Yin Earth	Snake	Feb	28	4:36
March 5–April 5	Yin Fire	Rabbit	Yin Earth	Snake	Mar	56	22:36
April 5–May 5	Yang Earth	Dragon	Yin Earth	Snake	April	27	3:39
May 5–June 6	Yin Earth	Snake	Yin Earth	Snake	May	57	21:13
June 6–July 7	Yang Metal	Horse	Yin Earth	Snake	June	28	1:35
July 7–August 7	Yin Metal	Sheep	Yin Earth	Snake	July	58	11:58
August 7–September 8	Yang Water	Monkey	Yin Earth	Snake	Aug	29	21:41
September 8–October 8	Yin Water	Cock	Yin Earth	Snake	Sep	60	1:07
October 8–ovember 7	Yang Wood	Dog	Yin Earth	Snake	Oct	30	15:49
November 7–December 7	Yin Wood	Pig	Yin Earth	Snake	Nov	1	19:59
December 7–January 5	Yang Fire	Rat	Yin Earth	Snake	Dec	31	11:24

Branch	Pig	Rat	Ox	Tiger	Rabbit	Dragon	Snake	Horse	Sheep	Monkey	Cock	Dog
Main Element	Yang Water	Yin Water	Yin Earth	Yang Wood	Yin Wood	Yang Earth	Yang Fire	Yang Fire	Yin Earth	Yang Metal	Yin Metal	Yang Earth
Hidden Elements	Yang Wood		Yin Water	Yang Fire		Yin Wood	Yang Earth	Yin Earth	Yin Fire	Yang Earth		Yin Metal
			Yin Metal	Yang Earth		Yin Water	Yang Metal		Yin Wood	Yang Water		Yin Fire

1990

Find your Day Here	Month Stem	Month Branch	Year Stem	Year Branch	Day	Day	Time
January 5–February 4	Yin Fire	Ox	Yin Earth	Snake	Jan	2	23:12
February 4–March 6	Yang Earth	Tiger	Yang Metal	Horse	Feb	33	10:15
March 6–April 5	Yin Earth	Rabbit	Yang Metal	Horse	Mar	1	4:25
April 5–May 6	Yang Metal	Dragon	Yang Metal	Horse	April	32	9:28
May 6–June 6	Yin Metal	Snake	Yang Metal	Horse	May	2	2:53
June 6–July 7	Yang Water	Horse	Yang Metal	Horse	June	33	7:24
July 7–August 8	Yin Water	Sheep	Yang Metal	Horse	July	3	17:47
August 8–September 8	Yang Wood	Monkey	Yang Metal	Horse	Aug	34	3:30
September 8–October 8	Yin Wood	Cock	Yang Metal	Horse	Sep	5	6:14
October 8–November 8	Yang Fire	Dog	Yang Metal	Horse	Oct	35	21:38
November 8–December 7	Yin Fire	Pig	Yang Metal	Horse	Nov	6	1:49
December 7–January 6	Yang Earth	Rat	Yang Metal	Horse	Dec	36	17:13

1991

Find your Day Here	Month Stem	Month Branch	Year Stem	Year Branch	Day	Day	Time
January 6–February 4	Yin Earth	Ox	Yang Metal	Horse	Jan	7	5:01
February 4–March 6	Yang Metal	Tiger	Yin Metal	Sheep	Feb	38	16:04
March 6–April 5	Yin Metal	Rabbit	Yin Metal	Sheep	Mar	6	10:14
April 5–May 6	Yang Water	Dragon	Yin Metal	Sheep	April	37	15:17
May 6–June 6	Yin Water	Snake	Yin Metal	Sheep	May	7	8:51
June 6–July 7	Yang Wood	Horse	Yin Metal	Sheep	June	38	13:14
July 7–August 8	Yin Wood	Sheep	Yin Metal	Sheep	July	8	23:37
August 8–September 8	Yang Fire	Monkey	Yin Metal	Sheep	Aug	39	9:20
September 8–October 9	Yin Fire	Cock	Yin Metal	Sheep	Sep	10	12:04
October 9–November 8	Yang Earth	Dog	Yin Metal	Sheep	Oct	4	3:28
November 8–December 8	Yin Earth	Pig	Yin Metal	Sheep	Nov	11	7:39
December 8–January 9	Yang Metal	Rat	Yin Metal	Sheep	Dec	41	:08

Branch	Pig	Rat	Ox	Tiger	Rabbit	Dragon	Snake	Horse	Sheep	Monkey	Cock	Dog
Main Element	Yang Water	Yin Water	Yin Earth	Yang Wood	Yin Wood	Yang Earth	Yang Fire	Yin Fire	Yin Earth	Yang Metal	Yin Metal	Yang Earth
Hidden Elements	Yang Wood		Yin Water	Yang Fire		Yin Wood	Yang Earth	Yin Earth	Yang Fire	Yang Earth		Yin Metal
			Yin Metal	Yang Earth		Yin Water	Yang Metal		Yin Wood	Yang Water		Yin Fire

1992

Find your Day Here	Month Stem	Branch	Year Stem	Branch	Day	Day	Time
January 9–February 7	Yin Metal	Ox	Yin Metal	Sheep	Jan	12	: 08
February 7–29,–March 7	Yang Water	Tiger	Yang Water	Monkey	Feb	43	10: 12
March 7–April 6	Yin Water	Rabbit	Yang Water	Monkey	Mar	12	21: 54
April 6–May 5	Yang Wood	Dragon	Yang Water	Monkey	April	43	16: 04
May 5–June 6	Yin Wood	Snake	Yang Water	Monkey	May	13	20: 57
June 6–July 7	Yang Fire	Horse	Yang Water	Monkey	June	44	14: 41
July 7–August 7	Yin Fire	Sheep	Yang Water	Monkey	July	14	18; 52
August 7–September 7	Yang Earth	Monkey	Yang Water	Monkey	Aug	45	5: 26
September 7–October 8	Yin Earth	Cock	Yang Water	Monkey	Sep	16	15: 09
October 8–November 7	Yang Metal	Dog	Yang Water	Monkey	Oct	46	17: 53
November 7–December 7	Yin Metal	Pig	Yang Water	Monkey	Nov	17	9: 17
December 7–January 5	Yang Water	Rat	Yang Water	Monkey	Dec	47	13: 28

1993

Find your Day Here	Month Stem	Branch	Year Stem	Branch	Day	Day	Time
January 5–February 4	Yin Water	Ox	Yang Water	Monkey	Jan	18	5: 58
February 4–March 5	Yang Wood	Tiger	Yin Water	Cock	Feb	49	16: 01
March 5–April 5	Yin Wood	Rabbit	Yin Water	Cock	Mar	17	3: 43
April 5–May 5	Yang Fire	Dragon	Yin Water	Cock	April	48	21: 53
May 5–June 6	Yin Fire	Snake	Yin Water	Cock	May	18	2: 56
June 6–July 7	Yang Earth	Horse	Yin Water	Cock	June	49	20: 30
July 7–August 7	Yin Earth	Sheep	Yin Water	Cock	July	19	11: 15
August 7–September 7	Yang Metal	Monkey	Yin Water	Cock	Aug	50	21: 10
September 7–October 8	Yin Metal	Cock	Yin Water	Cock	Sep	21	: 20
October 8–November 7	Yang Water	Dog	Yin Water	Cock	Oct	51	15: 07
November 7–December 8	Yin Water	Pig	Yin Water	Cock	Nov	22	19: 17
December 8–January 5	Yang Wood	Rat	Yin Water	Cock	Dec	52	11: 47

Branch	Pig	Rat	Ox	Tiger	Rabbit	Dragon	Snake	Horse	Sheep	Monkey	Cock	Dog
Main Element	Yang Water	Yin Water	Yin Earth	Yang Wood	Yin Wood	Yang Earth	Yang Fire	Yin Fire	Yin Earth	Yang Metal	Yin Metal	Yang Earth
Hidden Elements	Yang Wood		Yin Water	Yang Fire		Yin Wood	Yang Earth	Yin Earth	Yin Fire	Yang Earth		Yin Metal
			Yin Metal	Yang Earth		Yin Water	Yang Metal		Yin Wood	Yang Water		Yin Fire

1994

	Month		Year				
Find your Day Here	Stem	Branch	Stem	Branch	Day	Day	Time
January 5–February 4	Yin Wood	Ox	Yin Water	Cock	Jan	23	21: 57
February 4–March 6	Yang Fire	Tiger	Yang Wood	Dog	Feb	54	9: 33
March 6–April 5	Yin Fire	Rabbit	Yang Wood	Dog	Mar	22	3: 43
April 5–May 6	Yang Earth	Dragon	Yang Wood	Dog	April	53	8: 46
May 6–June 6	Yin Earth	Snake	Yang Wood	Dog	May	23	2: 20
June 6–July 7	Yang Metal	Horse	Yang Wood	Dog	June	54	6: 43
July 7–August 8	Yin Metal	Sheep	Yang Wood	Dog	July	24	16: 55
August 8–September 7	Yang Water	Monkey	Yang Wood	Dog	Aug	55	2: 50
September 8–October 8	Yin Water	Cock	Yang Wood	Dog	Sep	26	5: 34
October 8–November 7	Yang Wood	Dog	Yang Wood	Dog	Oct	56	22; 00
November 7–December 7	Yin Wood	Pig	Yang Wood	Dog	Nov	27	1: 06
December 7–January 6	Yang Fire	Rat	Yang Wood	Dog	Dec	57	17: 36

1995

	Month		Year				
Find your Day Here	Stem	Branch	Stem	Branch	Day	Day	Time
January 6–February 4	Yin Fire	Ox	Yang Wood	Dog	Jan	28	3: 42
February 4–March 6	Yang Earth	Tiger	Yin Wood	Pig	Feb	59	15: 24
March 6–April 5	Yin Earth	Rabbit	Yin Wood	Pig	Mar	27	9: 34
April 5–May 6	Yang Metal	Dragon	Yin Wood	Pig	April	58	14: 37
May 6–June 6	Yin Metal	Snake	Yin Wood	Pig	May	28	8: 11
June 6–July 7	Yang Water	Horse	Yin Wood	Pig	June	59	12: 34
July 7–August 8	Yin Water	Sheep	Yin Wood	Pig	July	29	22: 57
August 8–September 8	Yang Wood	Monkey	Yin Wood	Pig	Aug	60	22: 57
September 8–October 9	Yin Wood	Cock	Yin Wood	Pig	Sep	31	11: 25
October 9–November 8	Yang Fire	Dog	Yin Wood	Pig	Oct	1	3: 50
November 8–December 7	Yin Fire	Pig	Yin Wood	Pig	Nov	32	5: 44
December 7–January 6	Yang Earth	Rat	Yin Wood	Pig	Dec	2	23: 27

Branch	Pig	Rat	Ox	Tiger	Rabbit	Dragon	Snake	Horse	Sheep	Monkey	Cock	Dog
Main Element	Yang Water	Yin Water	Yin Earth	Yang Wood	Yin Wood	Yang Earth	Yang Fire	Yin Fire	Yin Earth	Yang Metal	Yin Metal	Yang Earth
Hidden Elements	Yang Wood		Yin Water	Yang Fire		Yin Wood	Yang Earth	Yin Earth	Yin Fire	Yang Earth		Yin Metal
			Yin Metal	Yang Earth		Yin Water	Yang Metal		Yin Wood	Yang Water		Yin Fire

1996

Find your Day Here	Month Stem	Branch	Year Stem	Branch	Day	Day	Time
January 6–February 4	Yin Earth	Ox	Yin Wood	Pig	Jan	33	9: 23
February 4–29,–March 5	Yang Metal	Tiger	Yang Fire	Rat	Feb	4	3: 26
March 5–April 4	Yin Metal	Rabbit	Yang Fire	Rat	Mar	33	15: 25
April 4–May 5	Yang Water	Dragon	Yang Fire	Rat	April	4	20: 28
May 5–June 5	Yin Water	Snake	Yang Fire	Rat	May	34	14: 02
June 5–July 7	Yang Wood	Horse	Yang Fire	Rat	June	5	18: 14
July 7–August 7	Yin Wood	Sheep	Yang Fire	Rat	July	35	4: 47
August 7–September 7	Yang Fire	Monkey	Yang Fire	Rat	Aug	6	14: 30
September 7–October 8	Yin Fire	Cock	Yang Fire	Rat	Sep	37	17: 14
October 8–November 7	Yang Earth	Dog	Yang Fire	Rat	Oct	7	9: 38
November 7–December 7	Yin Earth	Pig	Yang Fire	Rat	Nov	38	11: 32
December 7–January 5	Yang Metal	Rat	Yang Fire	Rat	Dec	8	5: 17

1997

Find your Day Here	Month Stem	Branch	Year Stem	Branch	Day	Day	Time
January 5–February 4	Yin Metal	Ox	Yang Fire	Rat	Jan	39	15: 22
February 4–March 5	Yang Water	Tiger	Yin Fire	Ox	Feb	10	3: 04
March 5–April 5	Yin Water	Rabbit	Yin Fire	Ox	Mar	38	21: 14
April 5–May 5	Yang Wood	Dragon	Yin Fire	Ox	April	9	2: 17
May 5–June 7	Yin Wood	Snake	Yin Fire	Ox	May	39	19: 50
June 7–July 7	Yang Fire	Horse	Yin Fire	Ox	June	10	23: 53
July 7–August 7	Yin Fire	Sheep	Yin Fire	Ox	July	40	10: 36
August 7–September 7	Yang Earth	Monkey	Yin Fire	Ox	Aug	11	20: 19
September 7–October 8	Yin Earth	Cock	Yin Fire	Ox	Sep	42	23: 03
October 8–November 7	Yang Metal	Dog	Yin Fire	Ox	Oct	12	15: 27
November 7–December 7	Yin Metal	Pig	Yin Fire	Ox	Nov	43	17: 22
December 7–January 5	Yang Water	Rat	Yin Fire	Ox	Dec	13	11: 05

Branch	Pig	Rat	Ox	Tiger	Rabbit	Dragon	Snake	Horse	Sheep	Monkey	Cock	Dog
Main Element	Yang Water	Yin Water	Yin Earth	Yang Wood	Yin Wood	Yang Earth	Yang Fire	Yin Fire	Yin Earth	Yang Metal	Yin Metal	Yang Earth
Hidden Elements	Yang Wood		Yin Water	Yang Fire		Yin Wood	Yang Earth	Yin Earth	Yin Fire	Yang Earth		Yin Metal
			Yin Metal	Yang Earth		Yin Water	Yang Metal		Yin Wood	Yang Water		Yin Fire

1998

	Month		Year				
Find your Day Here	Stem	Branch	Stem	Branch	Day	Day	Time
January 5–February 4	Yin Water	Ox	Yin Fire	Ox	Jan	44	21: 11
February 4–March 6	Yang Wood	Tiger	Yang Earth	Tiger	Feb	15	9: 05
March 6–April 5	Yin Wood	Rabbit	Yang Earth	Tiger	Mar	43	2: 57
April 5–May 6	Yang Fire	Dragon	Yang Earth	Tiger	April	14	8: 06
May 6–June 6	Yin Fire	Snake	Yang Earth	Tiger	May	44	1: 40
June 6–July 7	Yang Earth	Horse	Yang Earth	Tiger	June	15	6: 02
July 7–August 8	Yin Earth	Sheep	Yang Earth	Tiger	July	45	22: 44
August 8–September 8	Yang Metal	Monkey	Yang Earth	Tiger	Aug	16	16: 25
September 8–October 8	Yin Metal	Cock	Yang Earth	Tiger	Sep	47	5: 24
October 8–November 7	Yang Water	Dog	Yang Earth	Tiger	Oct	17	21: 16
November 7–December 7	Yin Water	Pig	Yang Earth	Tiger	Nov	48	: 24
December 7–January 6	Yang Wood	Rat	Yang Earth	Tiger	Dec	18	15: 51

1999

	Month		Year				
Find your Day Here	Stem	Branch	Stem	Branch	Day	Day	Time
January 6–February 4	Yin Wood	Ox	Yang Earth	Tiger	Jan	49	3: 00
February 4–March 6	Yang Fire	Tiger	Yin Earth	Rabbit	Feb	20	14: 42
March 6–April 5	Yin Fire	Rabbit	Yin Earth	Rabbit	Mar	48	8: 52
April 5–May 6	Yang Earth	Dragon	Yin Earth	Rabbit	April	19	13: 55
May 6–June 6	Yin Earth	Snake	Yin Earth	Rabbit	May	49	7: 29
June 6–July 7	Yang Metal	Horse	Yin Earth	Rabbit	June	20	11: 51
July 7–August 8	Yin Metal	Sheep	Yin Earth	Rabbit	July	50	22: 14
August 8–September 8	Yang Water	Monkey	Yin Earth	Rabbit	Aug	21	7: 57
September 8–October 9	Yin Water	Cock	Yin Earth	Rabbit	Sep	52	11: 13
October 9–November 7	Yang Wood	Dog	Yin Earth	Rabbit	Oct	22	3: 06
November 7–December 7	Yin Wood	Pig	Yin Earth	Rabbit	Nov	53	6: 14
December 7–January 6	Yang Fire	Rat	Yin Earth	Rabbit	Dec	23	21: 14

Branch	Pig	Rat	Ox	Tiger	Rabbit	Dragon	Snake	Horse	Sheep	Monkey	Cock	Dog
Main Element	Yang Water	Yin Water	Yin Earth	Yang Wood	Yin Wood	Yang Earth	Yang Fire	Yin Fire	Yin Earth	Yang Metal	Yin Metal	Yang Earth
Hidden Elements	Yang Wood		Yin Water	Yang Fire		Yin Wood	Yang Earth	Yin Earth	Yin Fire	Yang Earth		Yin Metal
			Yin Metal	Yang Earth		Yin Water	Yang Metal		Yin Wood	Yang Water		Yin Fire

2000

Find your Day Here	Month Stem	Branch	Year Stem	Branch	Day	Day	Time
January 6–February 4	Yin Fire	Ox	Yin Earth	Rabbit	Jan	54	9: 30
February 4–29,–March 5	Yang Earth	Tiger	Yang Metal	Dragon	Feb	25	20: 32
March 5–April 4	Yin Earth	Rabbit	Yang Metal	Dragon	Mar	54	14: 42
April 4–May 5	Yang Metal	Dragon	Yang Metal	Dragon	April	25	19: 45
May 5–June 5	Yin Metal	Snake	Yang Metal	Dragon	May	55	12: 58
June 5–July 7	Yang Water	Horse	Yang Metal	Dragon	June	26	17: 41
July 7–August 7	Yin Water	Sheep	Yang Metal	Dragon	July	56	4: 04
August 7–September 7	Yang Wood	Monkey	Yang Metal	Dragon	Aug	27	13: 36
September 7–October 8	Yin Wood	Cock	Yang Metal	Dragon	Sep	58	17: 01
October 8–November 7	Yang Fire	Dog	Yang Metal	Dragon	Oct	28	7: 56
November 7–December 7	Yin Fire	Pig	Yang Metal	Dragon	Nov	59	12: 03
December 7–January 5	Yang Earth	Rat	Yang Metal	Dragon	Dec	29	3: 29

2001

Find your Day Here	Month Stem	Branch	Year Stem	Branch	Day	Day	Time
January 5–February 4	Yin Earth	Ox	Yang Metal	Dragon	Jan	60	3: 19
February 4–March 5	Yang Meta	Tiger	Yin Metal	Snake	Feb	31	2: 20
March 5–April 5	Yin Metal	Rabbit	Yin Metal	Snake	Mar	59	20: 30
April 5–May 5	Yang Wate	Dragon	Yin Metal	Snake	April	30	1: 33
May 5–June 5	Yin Water	Snake	Yin Metal	Snake	May	60	18: 46
June 5–July 7	Yang Wood	Horse	Yin Metal	Snake	June	31	23: 29
July 7–August 7	Yin Wood	Sheep	Yin Metal	Snake	July	1	9: 52
August 7–September 7	Yang Fire	Monkey	Yin Metal	Snake	Aug	32	19: 34
September 7–October 8	Yin Fire	Cock	Yin Metal	Snake	Sep	3	22: 18
October 8–November 7	Yang Earth	Dog	Yin Metal	Snake	Oct	33	13: 42
November 7–December 7	Yin Earth	Pig	Yin Metal	Snake	Nov	4	17: 53
December 7–January 5	Yang Metal	Rat	Yin Metal	Snake	Dec	34	9: 17

Branch	Pig	Rat	Ox	Tiger	Rabbit	Dragon	Snake	Horse	Sheep	Monkey	Cock	Dog
Main Element	Yang Water	Yin Water	Yin Earth	Yang Wood	Yin Wood	Yang Earth	Yang Fire	Yin Fire	Yin Earth	Yang Metal	Yin Metal	Yang Earth
Hidden Elements	Yang Wood		Yin Water	Yang Fire		Yin Wood	Yang Earth	Yin Earth	Yin Fire	Yang Earth		Yin Metal
			Yin Metal	Yang Earth		Yin Water	Yang Metal		Yin Wood	Yang Water		Yin Fire

2002

Find your Day Here	Month Stem	Branch	Year Stem	Branch	Day	Day	Time
January 5–February 4	Yin Metal	Ox	Yin Metal	Snake	Jan	5	21: 10
February 4–March 6	Yang Water	Tiger	Yang Water	Horse	Feb	36	8: 08
March 6–April 5	Yin Water	Rabbit	Yang Water	Horse	Mar	4	2: 18
April 5–May 6	Yang Wood	Dragon	Yang Water	Horse	April	35	7: 21
May 6–June 6	Yin Wood	Snake	Yang Water	Horse	May	5	: 55
June 6–July 7	Yang Fire	Horse	Yang Water	Horse	June	36	4: 54
July 7–August 8	Yin Fire	Sheep	Yang Water	Horse	July	6	15: 40
August 8–September 8	Yang Earth	Monkey	Yang Water	Horse	Aug	37	1: 23
September 8–October 8	Yin Earth	Cock	Yang Water	Horse	Sep	8	4: 07
October 8–November 7	Yang Metal	Dog	Yang Water	Horse	Oct	38	19: 31
November 7–December 7	Yin Metal	Pig	Yang Water	Horse	Nov	9	23: 43
December 7–January 6	Yang Water	Rat	Yang Water	Horse	Dec	39	15: 16

2003

Find your Day Here	Month Stem	Branch	Year Stem	Branch	Day	Day	Time
January 6–February 4	Yin Water	Ox	Yang Water	Horse	Jan	10	2: 15
February 4–March 6	Yang Wood	Tiger	Yin Water	Sheep	Feb	41	13: 57
March 6–April 5	Yin Wood	Rabbit	Yin Water	Sheep	Mar	9	8; 07
April 5–May 6	Yang Fire	Dragon	Yin Water	Sheep	April	40	12: 55
May 6–June 6	Yin Fire	Snake	Yin Water	Sheep	May	10	6: 44
June 6–July 7	Yang Earth	Horse	Yin Water	Sheep	June	41	10: 42
July 7–August 8	Yin Earth	Sheep	Yin Water	Sheep	July	11	21: 29
August 8–September 8	Yang Metal	Monkey	Yin Water	Sheep	Aug	42	7: 12
September 8–October 9	Yin Metal	Cock	Yin Water	Sheep	Sep	13	9: 56
October 9–November 8	Yang Water	Dog	Yin Water	Sheep	Oct	43	1: 20
November 8–December 7	Yin Water	Pig	Yin Water	Sheep	Nov	14	5: 31
December 7–January 6	Yang Wood	Rat	Yin Water	Sheep	Dec	44	22: 04

Branch	Pig	Rat	Ox	Tiger	Rabbit	Dragon	Snake	Horse	Sheep	Monkey	Cock	Dog
Main Element	Yang Water	Yin Water	Yin Earth	Yang Wood	Yin Wood	Yang Earth	Yang Fire	Yin Fire	Yin Earth	Yang Metal	Yin Metal	Yang Earth
Hidden Elements	Yang Wood		Yin Water	Yang Fire		Yin Wood	Yang Earth	Yin Earth	Yin Fire	Yang Earth		Yin Metal
			Yin Metal	Yang Earth		Yin Water	Yang Metal		Yin Wood	Yang Water		Yin Fire

2004

Find your Day Here	Month		Year				
	Stem	Branch	Stem	Branch	Day	Day	Time
January 6–February 4	Yin Wood	Ox	Yin Water	Sheep	Jan	15	8:04
February 4–29,–March 5	Yang Fire	Tiger	Yang Wood	Monkey	Feb	46	19:46
March 5–April 4	Yin Fire	Rabbit	Yang Wood	Monkey	Mar	15	13:56
April 4–May 5	Yang Earth	Dragon	Yang Wood	Monkey	April	46	18:59
May 5–June 5	Yin Earth	Snake	Yang Wood	Monkey	May	16	12:33
June 5–July 7	Yang Metal	Horse	Yang Wood	Monkey	June	47	16:55
July 7–August 7	Yin Metal	Sheep	Yang Wood	Monkey	July	17	2:56
August 7–September 7	Yang Water	Monkey	Yang Wood	Monkey	Aug	48	13:00
September 7–October 8	Yin Water	Cock	Yang Wood	Monkey	Sep	19	15:44
October 8–November 7	Yang Wood	Dog	Yang Wood	Monkey	Oct	49	7:08
November 7–December 7	Yin Wood	Pig	Yang Wood	Monkey	Nov	20	11:21
December 7–January 5	Yang Fire	Rat	Yang Wood	Monkey	Dec	50	3:54

2005

Find your Day Here	Month		Year				
	Stem	Branch	Stem	Branch	Day	Day	Time
January 5–February 4	Yin Fire	Ox	Yang Wood	Monkey	Jan	21	13:52
February 4–March 5	Yang Earth	Tiger	Yin Wood	Cock	Feb	52	1:34
March 5–April 5	Yin Earth	Rabbit	Yin Wood	Cock	Mar	20	19:45
April 5–May 5	Yang Metal	Dragon	Yin Wood	Cock	April	51	:48
May 5–June 5	Yin Metal	Snake	Yin Wood	Cock	May	21	18:23
June 5–July 7	Yang Water	Horse	Yin Wood	Cock	June	52	22:45
July 7–August 7	Yin Water	Sheep	Yin Wood	Cock	July	22	8:44
August 7–September 7	Yang Wood	Monkey	Yin Wood	Cock	Aug	53	18:51
September 7–October 8	Yin Wood	Cock	Yin Wood	Cock	Sep	24	21:35
October 8–November 7	Yang Fire	Dog	Yin Wood	Cock	Oct	54	13:59
November 7–December 7	Yin Fire	Pig	Yin Wood	Cock	Nov	25	17:10
December 7–January 5	Yang Earth	Rat	Yin Wood	Cock	Dec	55	9:44

Branch	Pig	Rat	Ox	Tiger	Rabbit	Dragon	Snake	Horse	Sheep	Monkey	Cock	Dog
Main Element	Yang Water	Yin Water	Yin Earth	Yang Wood	Yin Wood	Yang Earth	Yang Fire	Yin Fire	Yin Earth	Yang Metal	Yin Metal	Yang Earth
Hidden Elements	Yang Wood		Yin Water	Yang Fire		Yin Wood	Yang Earth	Yin Earth	Yin Fire	Yang Earth		Yin Metal
			Yin Metal	Yang Earth		Yin Water	Yang Metal		Yin Wood	Yang Water		Yin Fire

2006

	Month		Year				
Find your Day Here	Stem	Branch	Stem	Branch	Day	Day	Time
January 5–February 4	Yin Earth	Ox	Yin Wood	Cock	Jan	26	20: 29
February 4–March 6	Yang Metal	Tiger	Yang Fire	Dog	Feb	57	7: 25
March 6–April 5	Yin Metal	Rabbit	Yang Fire	Dog	Mar	25	1: 35
April 5–May 5	Yang Water	Dragon	Yang Fire	Dog	April	56	6: 38
May 5–June 6	Yin Water	Snake	Yang Fire	Dog	May	26	23: 49
June 6–July 7	Yang Wood	Horse	Yang Fire	Dog	June	57	4: 34
July 7–August 8	Yin Wood	Sheep	Yang Fire	Dog	July	27	14: 57
August 8–September 8	Yang Fire	Monkey	Yang Fire	Dog	Aug	58	: 40
September 8–October 8	Yin Fire	Cock	Yang Fire	Dog	Sep	29	3: 32
October 8–November 7	Yang Earth	Dog	Yang Fire	Dog	Oct	59	19: 48
November 7–December 7	Yin Earth	Pig	Yang Fire	Dog	Nov	30	23: 00
December 7–January 6	Yang Metal	Rat	Yang Fire	Dog	Dec	60	15: 33

2007

	Month		Year				
Find your Day Here	Stem	Branch	Stem	Branch	Day	Day	Time
January 5–February 4	Yin Metal	Ox	Yang Fire	Dog	Jan	31	1: 32
February 4–March 6	Yang Water	Tiger	Yin Fire	Pig	Feb	2	13: 14
March 6–April 5	Yin Water	Rabbit	Yin Fire	Pig	Mar	30	7; 24
April 5–May 5	Yang Wood	Dragon	Yin Fire	Pig	April	1	12: 27
May 5–June 6	Yin Wood	Snake	Yin Fire	Pig	May	31	6: 01
June 6–July 7	Yang Fire	Horse	Yin Fire	Pig	June	2	10: 23
July 7–August 8	Yin Fire	Sheep	Yin Fire	Pig	July	32	20: 46
August 8–September 8	Yang Earth	Monkey	Yin Fire	Pig	Aug	3	6: 29
September 8–October 8	Yin Earth	Cock	Yin Fire	Pig	Sep	34	9: 13
October 8–November 7	Yang Metal	Dog	Yin Fire	Pig	Oct	4	1: 37
November 7–December 7	Yin Metal	Pig	Yin Fire	Pig	Nov	35	3: 32
December 7–January 6	Yang Water	Rat	Yin Fire	Pig	Dec	5	21: 23

Branch	Pig	Rat	Ox	Tiger	Rabbit	Dragon	Snake	Horse	Sheep	Monkey	Cock	Dog
Main Element	Yang Water	Yin Water	Yin Earth	Yang Wood	Yin Wood	Yang Earth	Yang Fire	Yin Fire	Yin Earth	Yang Metal	Yin Metal	Yang Earth
Hidden Elements	Yang Wood		Yin Water	Yang Fire		Yin Wood	Yang Earth	Yin Earth	Yin Fire	Yang Earth		Yin Metal
			Yin Metal	Yang Earth		Yin Water	Yang Metal		Yin Wood	Yang Water		Yin Fire

2008

	Month		Year				
Find your Day Here	Stam	Branch	Stem	Branch	Day	Day	Time
January 6–February 4	Yin Water	Ox	Yin Fire	Pig	Jan	36	7:21
February 4–29,–March 5	Yang Wood	Tiger	Yang Earth	Rat	Feb	7	19:03
March 5–April 4	Yin Wood	Rabbit	Yang Earth	Rat	Mar	36	13:13
April 4–May 5	Yang Fire	Dragon	Yang Earth	Rat	April	7	28:16
May 5–June 5	Yin Fire	Snake	Yang Earth	Rat	May	37	11:50
June 5–July 7	Yang Earth	Horse	Yang Earth	Rat	June	8	16:12
July 7–August 7	Yin Earth	Sheep	Yang Earth	Rat	July	38	2:35
August 7–September 7	Yang Metal	Monkey	Yang Earth	Rat	Aug	9	12:18
September 7–October 8	Yin Metal	Cock	Yang Earth	Rat	Sep	40	15:02
October 8–November 7	Yang Water	Dog	Yang Earth	Rat	Oct	10	7:26
November 7–December 7	Yin Water	Pig	Yang Earth	Rat	Nov	41	9:21
December 7–January 5	Yang Wood	Rat	Yang Earth	Rat	Dec	11	3:13

2009

	Month		Year				
Find your Day Here	Stam	Branch	Stem	Branch	Day	Day	Time
January 5–February 6	Yin Wood	Ox	Yang Earth	Rat	Jan	42	13:10
February 6–March 5	Yang Fire	Tiger	Yin Earth	Ox	Feb	13	1:12
March 5–April 4	Yin Fire	Rabbit	Yin Earth	Ox	Mar	41	19:02
April 4–May 5	Yang Earth	Dragon	Yin Earth	Ox	April	12	23:49
May 5–June 5	Yin Earth	Snake	Yin Earth	Ox	May	42	17:39
June 5–July 7	Yang Metal	Horse	Yin Earth	Ox	June	13	22:01
July 7–August 8	Yin Metal	Sheep	Yin Earth	Ox	July	43	8:24
August 8–September 7	Yang Water	Monkey	Yin Earth	Ox	Aug	14	18:07
September 7–October 8	Yin Water	Cock	Yin Earth	Ox	Sep	45	21:18
October 8–November 7	Yang Wood	Dog	Yin Earth	Ox	Oct	15	13:15
November 7–December 7	Yin Wood	Pig	Yin Earth	Ox	Nov	46	15:10
December 7–January 5	Yang Fire	Rat	Yin Earth	Ox	Dec	16	9:03

Branch	Pig	Rat	Ox	Tiger	Rabbit	Dragon	Snake	Horse	Sheep	Monkey	Cock	Dog
Main Element	Yang Water	Yin Water	Yin Earth	Yang Wood	Yin Wood	Yang Earth	Yang Fire	Yin Fire	Yin Earth	Yang Metal	Yin Metal	Yang Earth
Hidden Elements	Yang Wood		Yin Water	Yang Fire		Yin Wood	Yang Earth	Yin Earth	Yin Fire	Yang Earth		Yin Metal
			Yin Metal	Yang Earth		Yin Water	Yang Metal		Yin Wood	Yang Water		Yin Fire

2010

Find your Day Here	Month Stam	Branch	Year Stem	Branch	Day	Day	Time
January 5–February 4	Yin Fire	Ox	Yin Earth	Ox	Jan	47	19: 00
February 4–March 6	Yang Earth	Tiger	Yang Metal	Tiger	Feb	18	7: 01
March 6–April 5	Yin Earth	Rabbit	Yang Metal	Tiger	Mar	46	: 35
April 5–May 5	Yang Metal	Dragon	Yang Metal	Tiger	April	17	5: 55
May 5–June 6	Yin Metal	Snake	Yang Metal	Tiger	May	47	23: 29
June 6–July 7	Yang Water	Horse	Yang Metal	Tiger	June	18	3: 51
July 7–August 7	Yin Water	Sheep	Yang Metal	Tiger	July	48	14: 14
August 7–September 8	Yang Wood	Monkey	Yang Metal	Tiger	Aug	19	23: 57
September 8–October 8	Yin Wood	Cock	Yang Metal	Tiger	Sep	50	3: 04
October 8–November 7	Yang Fire	Dog	Yang Metal	Tiger	Oct	20	19: 04
November 7–December 7	Yin Fire	Pig	Yang Metal	Tiger	Nov	51	21: 01
December 7–January 6	Yang Earth	Rat	Yang Metal	Tiger	Dec	21	13: 41

Branch	Pig	Rat	Ox	Tiger	Rabbit	Dragon	Snake	Horse	Sheep	Monkey	Cock	Dog
Main Element	Yang Water	Yin Water	Yin Earth	Yang Wood	Yin Wood	Yang Earth	Yang Fire	Yin Fire	Yin Earth	Yang Metal	Yin Metal	Yang Earth
Hidden Elements	Yang Wood		Yin Water	Yang Fire		Yin Wood	Yang Earth	Yin Earth	Yin Fire	Yang Earth		Yin Metal
			Yin Metal	Yang Earth		Yin Water	Yang Metal		Yin Wood	Yang Water		Yin Fire

Four Pillars Chart

	Hour	Day	Month	Year
Stem Heavenly Influence				
Branch Main Element Heavenly Influence Hidden Element Heavenly Influence Hidden Element Heavenly Influence Hidden Element Heavenly Influence				

10 Year Luck Cycles

Age								
Stem Heavenly Influence								
Branch								
Main Element Heavenly Influence Hidden Element Heavenly Influence Hidden Element Heavenly Influence